P9-DNF-217

About the Author

◆ ◆ ◆

Michael C. McKenna, PhD, a former middle grades teacher, is now Professor of Reading at Georgia Southern University in Savannah. He visits schools almost every day and has long been interested in identifying teaching strategies that really work in challenging classrooms. He has published more than one hundred articles and seven books on various literacy topics. His research has been sponsored by the National Reading Research Center (NRRC) and the Center for the Improvement of Early Reading Achievement (CIERA).

Contents

◆ ◆ ◆

Introduction   1

SECTION 1
Decoding Strategies

Guiding Principles of Teaching Decoding   7
Phonics in the Upper Grades   9
Phonics Word Sorts   12
Tape-Recorded Text   17
Electronic Books   19

SECTION 2
Fluency Strategies

Guiding Principles of Teaching Fluency   25
Effective Fluency Methods   26
Classwide Peer Tutoring   30
Self-Selected Reading   31

SECTION 3
Vocabulary Strategies

Guiding Principles of Teaching Vocabulary   35
Feature Analysis   37
Graphic Organizers   45
Semantic Maps   59
Vocabulary Venns   62
Semantic Scales   64
List–Group–Label   66
Concept Sorts   68

Vocabulary Clusters   70
Silly Questions   78
Possible Sentences   80

SECTION 4
Comprehension Lesson Formats

Guiding Principles of Teaching Reading Comprehension   85
Directed Reading Activity   87
Directed Reading–Thinking Activity   88
K-W-L   90
Listen–Read–Discuss   94

SECTION 5
Questioning Strategies

Levels of Questions   97
Question–Answer Relationships   100
Question Clusters   103
Reciprocal Questioning   106
Questioning the Author   108

SECTION 6
Other Comprehension Strategies

Specific Skill Approaches   115
Walk-Throughs   116
Think-Alouds   118
Imaging   120
Teaching with Analogies   123
Charting New Territory   125
Guided Notes   130
Reading Guides   132
Anticipation Guides   137
Reciprocal Teaching   144
Guided Reading in Textual Settings   149
Summary Writing   153
Cloze Venns   157
Riddles   166
Puzzlers   180
20 More Ideas for Inferential Comprehension   188

SECTION 7
Suggested Professional Resources

Suggested Professional Resources   195

Index   198

Introduction

◆ ◆ ◆

UNDERSTANDING STRUGGLING READERS

Who, exactly, are the struggling readers in our classrooms? We know, to begin with, that there are many of them. For over three decades, the National Assessment of Educational Progress (NAEP) has painted a grim picture of the literacy challenges we face as teachers. In the year 2000, for example, 37% of fourth graders were judged to be reading below even a "basic" level of proficiency for their grade. These children differ demographically, linguistically, and culturally, of course, but they nevertheless share certain traits that can help us plan instruction feasibly. A useful perspective, and the one I have adopted in writing this volume, involves determining the developmental stage that struggling readers have reached and then providing instruction designed to carry them through it.

A STAGE PERSPECTIVE

As teachers, we can gain valuable insights into how to assist struggling readers by first considering the students who succeed. These normally developing readers pass through discernible stages on their way to proficiency. Based on the stages proposed by Jeanne Chall (1983/1996), we can describe their progress in broad terms.

A child begins to show signs of literate behavior during the *emergent literacy* period (not really a stage), beginning at birth and extending to about age 5. During this period, the child learns the alphabet, becomes familiar with storybooks and how print works, acquires an oral language foundation, and becomes aware of the recurring sounds heard in spoken words. All of these are prerequisites to learning to read.

At the *decoding* stage, beginning either in kindergarten or first grade, the child learns letter–sound relationships. In addition, a good many words are learned so well that they can be pronounced at sight, and many more can be analyzed on the basis of meaningful units such as prefixes, suffixes, and roots. During this stage, pronouncing most words is still laborious and time-consuming.

It is in the *fluency* stage, typically beginning at about second grade, that the recognition of most words becomes much quicker, to the point of being automatic. Reading fluency permits us to direct conscious thought to comprehending what we read. If we lack fluency, we must attend to words at the expense of meaning; once we attain it, reading becomes a very different experience.

Beginning at about grade three, normally developing children enter the stage that Chall describes as *"learning the new."* Now that less attention is required for word recognition, more of the child's mental resources can be devoted to comprehension. The child now begins to acquire information from text, and the strategies for doing so become more sophisticated with experience.

Chall's stage model does not end here, but teachers of struggling readers in the upper elementary and middle grades would consider it a great victory if their students progressed to the stage of learning the new. They would then be prepared to meet most high school reading expectations, not to mention the vast majority of workplace literacy demands.

There is far more to knowing about these stages than the fact that they tell us what might have been. The stage model provides a frame of reference that enables us to plan instruction according to the level that our students have reached. It is usually rather easy to identify the stage at which their reading development has been arrested. Spear-Swerling and Sternberg (1996) describe these children as having gotten "off track," stranded at an earlier developmental stage and unable to make significant progress until they successfully pass through that stage and into the next. It is not possible to leapfrog one of the stages, although it may be possible to accelerate through it in order to catch up.

THREE STRUGGLING READERS

The brief sketches that follow are composite descriptions of real children (McKenna & Robinson, 2002). Each of them presents characteristics typical of a student who has gotten off track at a particular stage of reading development.

> *Josh* struggles to pronounce unfamiliar words. He sometimes guesses at them and sometimes attempts to sound them out from left to right. His pace is plodding and uncertain. He does, however, know a fair number of words by sight, and whenever he encounters one of them he can pronounce it immediately.

> *Latrelle* has a good store of words she recognizes at sight, and she can successfully pronounce almost any unfamiliar word she encounters while reading. Her pace is

slow, however, and her oral reading is expressionless. She does not group words into meaningful phrases as she reads, and she tends to ignore punctuation.

Sean is a proficient oral reader, but when faced with new material he often has problems comprehending. This difficulty is especially evident when he is asked to read nonfiction and when he is expected to draw logical conclusions about what he reads. He is a fair student when new content is thoroughly explained by his teacher, but he has problems whenever he must learn it on his own from print.

Students like these represent the majority of struggling readers now enrolled in the upper elementary and middle grades. Based on these descriptions, you probably had no difficulty in categorizing these readers. Josh is still at the decoding stage. Latrelle has passed through the decoding stage but lacks fluency. Sean is a fluent oral reader who has yet to develop the comprehension strategies that will enable him to learn from nonfiction.

ASSESSMENT AND INSTRUCTION

Spear-Swerling and Sternberg suggest a two-step process for assisting struggling readers. The first step is to identify the stage of their present development. The second step is to provide instruction designed to carry them through that stage and into the next.

Determining a developmental stage is not especially difficult. Keep in mind that we are contending with very broad levels and are less concerned with the identification of specific skill deficits. Chall's stages are not clear-cut, of course, and merge into one another as students gain proficiency. It is nevertheless possible to characterize the needs of most struggling readers by means of the stage model. It is important to:

- ◆ Listen to the student read orally,
- ◆ Decide whether decoding is fluent or nonfluent, and
- ◆ Judge the student's ability to comprehend, especially when the material has been read aloud by the teacher (thereby removing the burden of decoding).

DESIGN OF THIS VOLUME

Helping teachers select appropriate instructional strategies is the aim of this book. Its design parallels the stage perspective, beginning with decoding strategies in Section 1, moving on to fluency strategies in Section 2, and finally to strategies effective in guiding and improving comprehension in Sections 3 through 6.

Of the numerous approaches and reproducibles presented in the following sections, the vast majority target vocabulary and comprehension. There are two reasons for this apparent imbalance. First, most of the struggling readers in the upper grades are at least relatively proficient decoders, although some linger at the decoding and fluency stages of development. Second, most of those who lack adequate decoding skills also lack comprehension strategies characteristic of more advanced reading stages. Consequently, the vocabulary and comprehension strategies included in this book should be useful with nearly all of the struggling readers you may encounter. Those students who are still at the decoding and fluency stages will require strategies drawn from more than one of the sections that follow.

READ MORE ABOUT IT

◆ ◆ ◆

Chall, Jeanne S. (1983/1996). *Stages of reading development*. New York: McGraw-Hill.

McKenna, Michael C., and Robinson, Richard D. (2002). *Teaching through text: A content literacy approach to content area reading* (3rd ed.). New York: Longman.

Spear-Swerling, Louise, and Sternberg, Robert J. (1996). *Off track: When poor readers become learning disabled*. Boulder, CO: Westview Press.

The nation's report card. (2000). National Center for Education Statistics, National Assessment for Educational Progress (NAEP), 1992–2000 Reading Assessments.

SECTION 1

◆ ◆ ◆

Decoding Strategies

Guiding Principles
of Teaching Decoding

◆ ◆ ◆

When decoding problems persist, a teacher may be tempted to focus on compensatory strategies such as context and sight words. These are inadequate, however. Unfortunately, there is no "magic bullet" for helping struggling readers acquire the decoding skills they need, and yet there are proven options from which to choose.

◆ *Do not assume that decoding instruction can be skipped.* Remember, there is no such thing as leapfrogging over any of the developmental stages, decoding included. Students still mired at this level need special assistance in order to make progress. Some teachers contend that compensatory skills, such as relying on context and sight words, can make up for a decoding deficit. This reasoning is flawed, however. Students cannot become proficient without grasping the alphabetic principle on which our language is based.

• *Do not ignore comprehension.* The need to focus on decoding does not mean that comprehension and vocabulary strategy instruction will be of no value; rather, it means that they must be supplemented by word recognition instruction as well.

• *Consider software applications.* Because these students are likely to comprise a relatively small portion of a class, software applications can also be an effective way of individualizing instruction. I highly recommend *Simon Sounds It Out*, published by Don Johnston. This sequential series of activities is in no way demeaning to older students and has been empirically validated with struggling middle schoolers. (I have no financial interest in this company but encourage you to examine their growing list of software for struggling readers. Visit their web site at www.donjohnston. com.)

• *Focus on spelling patterns.* Mature decoders do not "sound out" words letter by letter from left to right. They use familiar clusters of letters to streamline the process and make it more dependable. In particular, they look for rimes (letter combinations such as *-ate* and *-ide* that form the basis of rhyming words) to help them pronounce un-familiar words containing these familiar patterns (words like *create* and *collide*). (By the way, the spelling of *rime* is now accepted as a way of avoiding confusion with the poetic device.) The goal in instructing struggling readers in decoding is to bring them as quickly as possible to the point at which they can recognize such patterns and use them instantly while reading. The teaching strategies described in this section are aimed at achieving this goal.

Phonics in the Upper Grades

◆ ◆ ◆

A recent study at Vanderbilt University revealed that a significant number of struggling readers in middle schools still lack basic decoding skills. There was a time when educators addressed this serious problem by sidestepping phonics in the hope that they might provide such students with ways of compensating. "After all," they argued, "phonics has been tried and it hasn't worked." You may have heard this same argument.

Unfortunately, there is no way to leapfrog, or bypass, the decoding stage of reading development. Sooner or later each person endeavoring to read English must come to understand how the written language represents the sounds of speech. Generally, this happens as the child passes from (1) outright guessing at words to (2) trying to sound them out sequentially ("cuh"–"ah"–"tuh") to (3) using rhyming patterns from familiar words ("cuh"–"at"—"cat!"). Most middle schoolers still struggling with decoding know basic letter–sound relationships but lack strategies for attacking unfamiliar words when they encounter them.

COMPARE–CONTRAST

One of the most effective research-based strategies is what Pat Cunningham calls compare–contrast, or decoding by analogy with known words. The strategy works like this for one-syllable words:

Step	Example
1. The student runs into an unfamiliar word.	vat
2. The student locates the vowel and checks to see whether the vowel and the consonant or consonant cluster that follows it are part of a familiar word.	cat

9

3. The student removes the beginning consonant or consonants   -at
   (called the word's *onset*) from the familiar word.

4. The student mentally attaches the onset of the unfamiliar word   v - at
   and pronounces it in two chunks.

Compare–contrast can be easily taught. Familiar words containing useful rimes are often placed on the board for easy reference. There are several ways of displaying such words by exhibiting them on the wall.

WORD WALLS

One approach to creating a word wall is to compile columns of words, each column devoted to the same rime family. (I asked one little girl why she thought they were called families and she said simply, "Because they all have the same last name"!) A word wall created in this way would look like this:

at	*it*	*ug*	*eck*	*ot*	*ile*
cat	bit	bug	deck	cot	file
hat	fit	dug	heck	dot	mile
bat	hit	hug	neck	got	Nile
fat	kit	jug	peck	hot	pile
mat	lit	lug	wreck	jot	rile
pat	mit	mug		lot	tile
rat	pit	rug		not	while
sat	sit	tug		pot	
that	wit			rot	

Such a wall requires a good bit of board space and works best for students with little knowledge of riming patterns.

A second way of creating a word wall is to use only one familiar word from each family and to organize it by vowel. Here is how a word wall would look if you used the 37 most useful rimes:

a	*e*	*i*	*o*	*u*
back	pet	kick	hot	but
pat	meat	sing	hop	dunk
date	tell	hide	for	duck
fan	rest	pink	more	bump
saw		night	lock	bug
main		lip	woke	
bank		pill		
day		fir		
cake		pin		
nap		mice		

tale	fine
cash	
fall	
game	

This approach to a word wall was popularized at the Benchmark School in Pennsylvania. It lends itself well to the compare–contrast approach. Let's assume again that a student is having difficulty with the word *vat*. This dialogue shows how such a wall might be used.

TEACHER: What's the vowel?

STUDENT: *a*.

TEACHER: Can you find a word on the wall with *-at*?

STUDENT: *cat*.

TEACHER: Right! And if you take off the *c* and replace it with *v*, what do you get?

STUDENT: *vat*.

For multisyllabic words, the strategy involves taking one syllable at a time. It doesn't always work and it can be cumbersome, but it moves children toward the decoding strategy that fluent readers unconsciously use. This is why it's so effective. For example, when you see the nonsense word *zat*, the pronunciation just pops into your head even though you've never seen it before. You certainly did not sound it out letter by letter! Unconsciously, you contrasted it with words like *cat* and *bat* that contain the *-at* rime. That's precisely what we want our students to do.

READ MORE ABOUT IT

◆ ◆ ◆

Bear, Donald R., Invernizzi, Marcia, Templeton, Shane, and Johnston, Francine. (2000). *Words their way: Word study for phonics, vocabulary, and spelling instruction* (2nd ed.). Upper Saddle River, NJ: Prentice Hall.

Cunningham, Patricia M. (2000). *Phonics they use: Words for reading and writing* (3rd ed.). New York: HarperCollins.

Cunningham, Patricia M., and Allington, Richard L. (1999). *Classrooms that work: They can all read and write* (2nd ed.). New York: HarperCollins.

Cunningham, Patricia M., and Hall, Dottie P. (1994). *Making words*. Parsippany, NJ: Good Apple. [more than one volume now available]

Cunningham, Patricia M., and Hall, Dottie P. (1994). *Making big words*. Parsippany, NJ: Good Apple. [More than one volume now available]

Cunningham, Patricia M., and Hall, Dottie P. (1998). *Month-by-month phonics for upper grades*. Greensboro, NC: Carson-Dellosa.

Fry, Edward B., Kress, Jacqueline E., and Fountoukidis, Dona L. (2000). *The reading teacher's book of lists* (4th ed.). Upper Saddle River, NJ: Prentice Hall. [Excellent source of rime word lists]

Phonics Word Sorts

◆ ◆ ◆

Phonics word sorts are activities that require students to place words into categories based on some shared feature related to pronunciation, spelling, or word structure. Word sorts of this kind are not about word meanings (as in concept sorts). They concern only the physical features of words—their sight and sound. Phonics word sorts can be very simple, stressing a single characteristic. List 1 focuses on initial consonant sounds, List 2 on rimes. Students might group these words on that basis:

List 1	List 2
fact	sue
candy	date
call	true
first	due
foul	fate
could	gate

The same tasks become more challenging when alternate spellings are used. It is no longer just a matter of visual matching:

List 3	List 4
fat	glue
came	two
corn	hate
key	eight
chemistry	moo
farmer	wait
phone	do

Students looking for the same initial consonant sounds would rearrange the words in List 3 to form these lists:

fat	came
farmer	corn
phone	key
	chemistry

From the words in List 4, they would create these two lists of rhyming words, which are deceptive because of their spelling:

glue	hate
two	eight
moo	wait
do	

Struggling readers may perceive the sorting task as worthier of them, and certainly more interesting than the "spit-and-sputter" approaches that may not have served them well in the primary grades. In fact, even struggling students in the upper elementary and middle grades should be ready to sort longer words on a variety of characteristics. The words in List 5 can be grouped in several ways.

List 5		
goodness	affordable	rethink
untie	pretest	together
banker	comet	Michigan
about	submarine	disagreeing
agreement	unfriendly	wonderful

One way of sorting these words is on the basis of the number of syllables each contains. Given the following headings, the students regroup the words by pronouncing them:

2 Syllables	3 Syllables	4 Syllables
goodness	agreement	affordable
untie	submarine	disagreeing
banker	unfriendly	
about	together	
pretest	Michigan	
comet	wonderful	
rethink		

Another way to sort these same words stresses their structure. Asking students to look for affixes leads to a very different result:

Only a Prefix	Only a Suffix	No Prefix, No Suffix	Prefix and Suffix
untie	goodness	about	unfriendly
pretest	banker	comet	disagreeing
rethink	agreement	together	
submarine	wonderful	Michigan	
affordable			

OPEN AND CLOSED WORD SORTS

The directions you give to students can lead to very different sorting behaviors. For example, if you show the students List 1 and ask them to group the words by initial consonant sound, their task is straightforward and well defined. They know just what they are looking for. This task has been called a closed word sort (Gillet & Kita, 1979). But imagine giving them List 6 and simply requesting that they sort them *somehow*.

List 6
dead
how
bead
head
show
now
lead
brow
cow
plead
low
bread

One option would be to sort the words by spelling pattern, another to sort by rime. These strategies lead to very different results in this instance:

Option 1		Option 2			
dead	how	dead	bead	how	show
bead	show	head	plead	now	low
head	now	lead		brow	
lead	brow	bread		cow	
plead	cow				
bread	low				

Open word sorts challenge students to be inventive and to look for common features without being told in advance what those features are.

SUGGESTIONS FOR PLANNING WORD SORTS

Look to students' writing for clues about which words to include in sorts. Spelling is an excellent source of evidence about a student's understanding of letter–sound correspondences. Don't just "red pencil" errors, jot some of them down for inclusion in sorts.

Write the words on note cards so that manipulation by students is easier. In working with a whole class, note cards can be placed in a pocket chart for quick rearrangement. Ideally, each student, pair of students, or small group will have a deck of word cards that can be shuffled for additional study.

Try to limit your list to words that students can pronounce. Doing so will enable them to focus more easily on shared orthographic features. To help ensure that the words are familiar, pronounce them one by one at the beginning of the lesson as the words are displayed.

Donald Bear and his colleagues (Bear et al., 2000) suggest that exceptions not be hidden. In the words that follow, for instance, the final *e* makes the preceding vowel long in every case but one: *cake, hide, pale, sane, come, code*. Exceptions, or "oddballs," like the word *come* can be placed in a separate category.

Word card decks will grow as new patterns are explored. Portions of these decks can be used to conduct periodic reviews. These review sessions should be frequent but brief. An important goal should be increased speed of sorting by your students.

TEACHING VARIATIONS

Whether a word sort is open or closed, you can modify and vary the activity in several ways. Here are a few possibilities.

- Once the students have sorted the words in the original list, ask them to add more words (not on the list) that possess the feature shared by the words in each of the lists they have created. They may need to use a dictionary to see whether some of their candidate words are really words.
- Let students work with partners or in small teams. Not only will they find the activity more appealing, but you can vary the type of sort some of the teams undertake, depending on their needs.
- Ask the students to work individually as they do the initial sort. Then allow them to work in pairs or teams as they add new words to each of the lists they've created.
- Have students maintain a notebook in which the sorted words are kept. Review the contents with the students from time to time.
- If you are working with a single student or a small group, write each word on an

index card in advance. The sorting then involves physically arranging the cards. The manipulatives provide a hands-on experience, and the time required for students to copy the words is saved.

READ MORE ABOUT IT
◆ ◆ ◆

Bear, Donald R., Invernizzi, Marcia, Templeton, Shane, and Johnston, Francine. (2000). *Words their way: Word study for phonics, vocabulary, and spelling instruction* (2nd ed.). Upper Saddle River, New Jersey: Prentice Hall.

Cunningham, Patricia M. (2000). *Phonics they use: Words for reading and writing* (3rd ed.). New York: Longman.

Gillet, J., and Kita, M. J. (1979). Words, kids, and categories. *The Reading Teacher, 32,* 538–542.

Tape-Recorded Text

◆ ◆ ◆

Tape recording reading selections is frequently recommended as a means of assisting students who cannot independently read assigned materials. The rationale is that if they will follow along in the printed version while listening as it is read to them orally, their comprehension ability will not be hindered by their limited decoding.

PROCEDURE

The most obvious approach to tape recording—that of producing a verbatim oral version and providing it to those students the teacher believes might benefit—misses an opportunity to comment editorially, helping the student not only to recognize words but to process the text as well. Deshler and Graham (1980) recommend the following guidelines in preparing a tape:

1. Identify instructional goals and objectives.
2. Consider which portions of the selection relate to the objectives.
3. If portions are skipped, they should be summarized to build a context for the portions that actually are read aloud.
4. Distinguish important ideas from details.
5. Mention embedded aids (maps, charts, headings, tables, etc.).
6. Provide a system that enables the student to easily keep the correct place in the text while listening (e.g., referring to page numbers or subheadings as they are reached).

VARIATIONS

Many variations have been explored, such as allowing superior students to produce tapes and using the tapes in tandem with study guides. Many others are possible.

ADVANTAGES

Taped selections permit a degree of individualization without a great deal of class time being devoted to the student experiencing difficulty. Tapes are portable, copyable, and inexpensive. Once a "master" has been produced, it will serve the teacher until newer materials are adopted. In addition, when the selection to be read is a well-known literary work, professionally produced tapes may be available.

LIMITATIONS

Taping takes time and thoughtful effort. While other individuals, such as paraprofessionals and students, may be able to produce a verbatim recording, the teacher remains the ideal person to do the taping because of the benefits to be gained by departing from the text occasionally in order to summarize or comment. Good grounding in the content is necessary to break from the text in this way. There may also be a tendency to rely too heavily on this technique—to simply assume that it is working and to put the student out of one's thoughts. Also, this technique will not assist all students who suffer from severe decoding problems because it requires reasonably good listening skills on the part of the student plus the intent to comprehend and the ability to attend for more than a few minutes at a time.

VALIDATION

Taping has been shown to be an effective approach with some reading-disabled students. Rivers (1980) reported good results when students followed along in their textbooks while listening and when the tape began with a review of previous material. Schumaker, Deshler, and Denton (1982) found that disabled students were significantly assisted when (1) recordings prompted active student interaction and (2) direct instruction and review followed the listening session. Poor results were obtained, however, when students merely listened to the tapes with no availability of the text. The technique appears to show early promise when care is taken to involve the student and tailor the material.

READ MORE ABOUT IT
◆ ◆ ◆

Deshler, D. D., and Graham, S. (1980). Tape recording educational materials for secondary handicapped students. *Teaching Exceptional Children, 12,* 52–54.

Rivers, L. E. (1980). Use a tape recorder to teach basic skills. *Social Studies, 71*(4),171–174.

Schumaker, J. B., Deshler, D. D., and Denton, P. H. (1982). *An integrated system for providing content to LD adolescents using an audio-taped format* (Research Report No. 66). Lawrence, KS: University of Kansas Institute for Research in Learning Disabilities.

Electronic Books

◆ ◆ ◆

Computerized print offers important advantages to struggling readers who have limited decoding skills or who have not yet attained fluency. In many cases, electronic text is equipped with a listening version so that students can hear it read aloud as they follow along on the screen. Also, students can often access the pronunciation of individual words on demand by pointing and clicking. This feature is called "supported text" and enables readers to read material that is at their listening level of comprehension—material that would be frustrating or impossible to read without support. In a sense, the computer acts as a fluent reader who is also available to help out. What's more, there is never any embarrassment or distraction in asking for help.

Research suggests that reading electronic books with supported text results not only in better comprehension but also in improved fluency and sight word knowledge as well. These are by-products that will assist the student indirectly.

Electronic books can be purchased commercially. For example, the Start-to-Finish series of adapted classics, published by Don Johnston (www.donjohnston.com), has been independently validated with struggling middle grade readers (Hasselbring, 1999). Electronic text can also be constructed by teachers using special software. For example, WordPerfect and AppleWorks feature a pronunciation option allowing a teacher to type or scan any text into a word processing document, which can then be read, with synthesized pronunciation support, by students who visit a computer station where the document is displayed.

Here are some guidelines for using electronic text, whether it is commercially produced or teacher-made.

1. Know your software. Understand how it's structured, what options it offers, what support features it has. And above all, read the book yourself!

2. Know your goals. Most electronic books have listening options. If your aim is an automated read-aloud, that's easy. If you expect kids to actually read at a station or center, that's harder. *The rest of these suggestions are offered with the latter goal in mind.*

3. Aim for the listening level. One of the amazing implications of electronic books is that the "distance" between the independent reading level and the listening comprehension level is all but eliminated. As long as kids can access the pronunciation of any word, decoding does not have to stand in their way. Consequently, a wide range of materials is viable—you're not limited to books they can read independently.

4. Create an environment. Decide how and where to position the microcomputer, whether to use headsets (usually a good idea to limit noise pollution), and which other materials might be useful. For example, the software cover (generally attractive), a print copy of the book, and possibly other volumes by the same author can add appeal. Written student comments and reviews, posted at the center, can help build a community of literates.

5. Communicate your expectations. Kids must know that they are expected to read the text, and they must know how to get the digitized support they may need to do so. Take some time to establish procedures. I find it useful to suggest that really poor decoders use the hand-and-finger icon to keep their place. That way, they're ready to click on words they need help with. This also provides a means for you to monitor them.

6. Prepare your students for each book. Consider whether the book requires an advance introduction for some students. Most books are so supportive with audio and pictures that few problems will be encountered, however. Words likely to challenge decoding ability need not be previewed, of course, since pronunciations will be available on demand. But words that represent unfamiliar concepts may require attention in advance. If students will rotate through a center, simply plan a brief whole-class introduction to the book.

7. Monitor for problems. Eavesdrop over shoulders to ensure that kids are actually making their way through the text—word by word and line by line—as you'd expect them to in a print book.

8. Monitor for comprehension. If a book is to be read for the first time, provide some means of checking to ensure that the kids have understood it. You can ask a question orally once they've finished, you can place a written question at the center and ask for a written answer, or you can arrange for a personalized response to the book. These are only a few ideas, of course.

9. Let them play. Electronic books that offer a "play" option (e.g., Broderbund's "Living Books") cannot be denied. From dancing starfish to singing flowers, let kids exhaust the possibilities through exploration. Then have them get down to the business of actually reading the book.

10. Limit pronunciations to single words. The best environments for learning new words while reading electronic books are those in which all pronunciations are available, but one word at a time. Software that repeats an entire line, or highlights phrases as they're read by a narrator, no doubt supports comprehension, but few sight words are likely to be acquired in this fashion. It's simply too difficult for a child to look at a word at the exact moment it's pronounced. (Try it yourself sometime!) But when the child points and clicks, the eyes are in the right place at the right time to take advantage of the look–say effect. Our studies clearly show that words are learned through incidental exposure in this way.

11. Couple electronic books with other learning. Where links are clear, tie the books kids read in electronic settings to topics they encounter in science, social studies, and math. Even incidental mention can reinforce content learning. And remember that a link to writing is always a viable possibility.

12. Create your own books. Software now enables you to create supported text simply by keyboarding or scanning it in. The result is usually a bare-bones product, but one that is free of distractions and easy to create, modify, and replace. You can even embed a question or editorial comment here and there. Such software also presents an exciting means by which students can publish their own writing to share with classmates.

13. Consider authoring software. You can make your own talking books (and any other text, for that matter) by using software that automatically provides pronunciation support on demand. One example is the CAST e-Reader, created by the Center for Applied Special Technology (www.cast.org) and marketed by Don Johnston.

SUGGESTED AUTHORING SOFTWARE

Intellitalk, published by Intellitools
 www.intellitools.com
Write Out Loud, published by Don Johnston
 www.donjohnston.com
AppleWorks, by Apple Computers
 www.apple.com
Ultimate E-Reader, published by Don Johnston
 www.donjohnston.com
Word Perfect, by IBM
 www.ibm.com

READ MORE ABOUT IT
◆ ◆ ◆

McKenna, Michael C. (1998). Electronic texts and the transformation of beginning reading. In D. Reinking, M. C. McKenna, L. D. Labbo, and R. Kieffer (Eds.), *Handbook of literacy and technology: Transformations in a posttypographic world* (pp. 45–59). Hillsdale, NJ: Erlbaum.

McKenna, Michael C., Reinking, D., and Labbo, L. D. (1997). Using talking books with reading-disabled students. *Reading and Writing Quarterly, 13,* 185–190.

SECTION 2

◆ ◆ ◆

Fluency Strategies

Guiding Principles
of Teaching Fluency

◆ ◆ ◆

Many readers in the upper elementary and middle grades can decode nearly any word, given enough time. But time is of the essence, and so is memory. When we spend too much time and attention figuring out individual words, we are hard-pressed to bring meaning to our reading. Fluency is all about speed. The faster and more automatically one can decode words, the more mental resources become available for comprehension. It's a simple relationship.

Readers who are reasonably good at decoding but continue to lack fluency are easy to spot. Their reading is often halting, they may pause in the wrong places, and not pause in the places they should. Until they become fluent, comprehension is likely to suffer.

◆ *Do not assume that fluency instruction can be skipped.* As in the case of decoding, there can be no leapfrogging over the fluency stage. Students still stuck at this level require assistance in order to become fluent.

◆ *Practice, practice, practice!* There's an old joke in which a young man asks a hip New Yorker how to get to Carnegie Hall. "Practice, man, practice," the New Yorker replies. The same advice will lead a reader to fluency, for the key is definitely practice. The more students read, the more fluent they become, and providing opportunities for reading materials written at an appropriate difficulty level is the principal means to this end.

◆ *Maximize the time spent reading.* The strategies described in this section are designed to maximize the time that students actually spend reading. Like all of the strategies described in this book, they are research-based and almost sure to be effective given adequate time to work.

◆ *Model fluent reading.* By reading aloud to students, you can model the rhetorical rhythms of appropriate oral language. Observing punctuation and altering inflection show students how fluent reading reflects meaning. This approach can send a subtle message about how our language communicates thoughts.

Effective Fluency Methods

♦ ♦ ♦

Fluency consists of (1) rapid, automatic word recognition and (2) phrasing and intonation that reflect the meaning of what is read. The key to attaining fluency can be summed up in one word: *practice*. Teachers must examine their schedules and their instructional techniques to look for ways of maximizing the time students spend actually reading. Several methods have proved especially effective in helping students attain fluency.

REPEATED READINGS

Students read the same material more than once, either during the same session or over a period of days. Each repetition leads to greater speed, which can be measured and tracked on a chart if desired. Sight words are acquired incidentally, and phrasing improves as the student's confidence grows.

PAIRED READING

Students are paired and read orally to each other. This is preferable to round-robin oral reading because each student spends half the allotted time reading instead of a small fraction.

PAIRED REPEATED READING

Students read the *same material* to each other. For example, if a stronger and weaker reader are paired, the stronger may read a paragraph to the weaker and then the weaker reads the same paragraph back to the better reader.

CLOCK PARTNERS

Both in paired reading and paired repeated reading, the teacher must decide how students are to be matched up. What is the best way to choose partners? Several methods are in common use, and all of them have their advocates. For example,

1. *Good reader–poor reader.* The logic of this approach is that the abler student will support the struggling student. This assistance can take many forms, one of which is described above.
2. *Just friends.* Some teachers report success through allowing students to select their own partner. This method may invite social problems, of course, such as talkative pairs and solitary students.
3. *Leveled pairs.* Students reading at about the same general level can be paired. This system prevents abler students from assisting struggling readers, but it does allow pairs to work on selections at an appropriate level of difficulty.

An alternative to these approaches is to create "clock partners." Each student receives a 3" x 5" card with a handless clockface stamped on it. (Most print shops stock this image for rubber stamps.) Other students' names are written at various hours, though not necessarily at all 12 hours. For example, each student may have a 12 o'clock partner, a 3 o'clock partner, a 6 o'clock partner, and a 9 o'clock partner. A completed card might look like this:

To ensure a variety of partners, it is probably best for the teacher to complete the cards before they are distributed to the students. However, an alternative is to begin by explaining to the students that they are to walk about the room, asking other students to be their clock partners. In this approach the teacher must ensure that everyone has a partner for each of the hours decided upon (I recommend 12, 3, 6, and 9 to begin with). It goes without saying that the cards must agree. If Ben is Jane's 3 o'clock partner, then Jane must also be Ben's 3 o'clock partner.

Clock partners add an element of variety to classroom activities, and not merely oral reading practice sessions. Pairing for any purpose might be done through clock partners. A teacher might distribute a science worksheet and tell the students to find their 6 o'clock partner, for example, or ask students to sit with their 9 o'clock partner to review spelling words before a test.

One advantage of the teacher assigning clock partners is that different pairings might be used for different purposes. For example, the 12 o'clock pairings might bring good and poor readers together while the 3 o'clock pairings might link students with common reading interests. When the teacher wants to conduct a paired repeated readings session, the 12 o'clock partners would meet, but a session designed to allow book sharing might involve the 3 o'clock partners.

On the following page, you will find a page of reproducible clock partner cards. You may copy them onto plain or stock paper. Of course, you may prefer to purchase your own stamp!

MORE FLUENCY METHODS

Here are a few more instructional strategies that might lend variety as you seek to develop oral fluency.

1. *Plays*. Students assume roles and read them aloud in class. Plays emphasize good intonation and phrasing (sometimes called prosody). Rehearsals also embody repeated readings.
2. *Echo reading*. Students repeat (echo) what the teacher reads aloud, usually one sentence or phrase at a time.
3. *Choral reading*. Students read aloud with the teacher, simultaneously. This approach is good for a change of pace but is hard to monitor.

READ MORE ABOUT IT
◆ ◆ ◆

Opitz, Michael F., Rasinski, Timothy F., and Bird, Lois Bridges. (1998). *Good-bye round robin: 25 effective oral reading strategies*. Westport, CT: Heinemann.

Rasinski, Timothy V., and Padak, Nancy. (2000). *From phonics to fluency: Effective teaching of decoding and reading fluency in the elementary school*. New York: Longman.

Topping, Keith. (1995). *Paired reading, spelling and writing: The handbook for teachers and parents*. New York: Cassell.

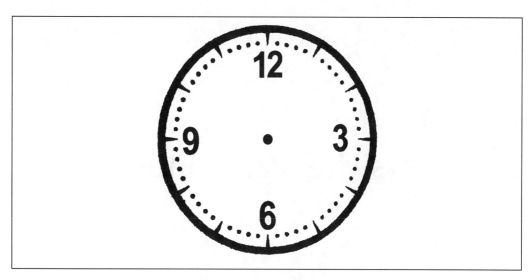

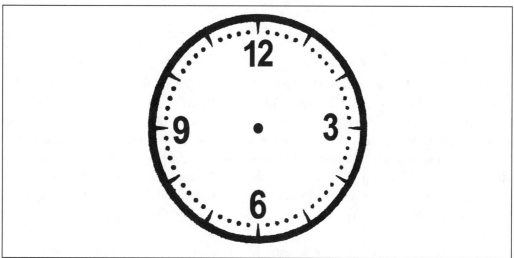

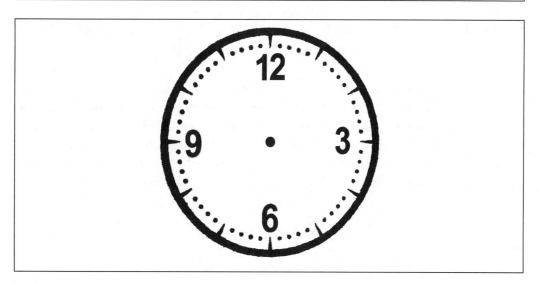

From *Help for Struggling Readers* by Michael C. McKenna. Copyright 2002 by The Guilford Press. Permission to photocopy this page is granted to purchasers of this book for personal use only (see copyright page for details).

Classwide Peer Tutoring

◆ ◆ ◆

Classwide peer tutoring (CWPT) originated in the 1970s with the Juniper Garden Children's Project as a technique aimed at helping urban teachers contend with challenging children. The idea is to increase student involvement in learning. Each week, every student is paired with another student, and each pair is assigned to one of two teams. Any reading materials can be used, including a basal reader. The tutee usually reads orally for about 10 minutes while the tutor monitors the reading, correcting errors. For the next five minutes the tutor asks questions about what the tutee has read. The roles are then reversed. Let's sum up the components of each 30-minute lesson:

10 minutes	Team 1 child in each pair reads aloud as Team 2 child monitors.
5 minutes	Team 1 child asks comprehension questions.
10 minutes	Team 2 child in each pair reads aloud as Team 1 child monitors.
5 minutes	Team 2 child asks comprehension questions.

The child who is not reading keeps score for his partner as follows: 2 points for reading a sentence without errors, 1 point for self-correcting an error. Errors include substitutions, omissions, and hesitations. At week's end, points are tallied. Each student's score includes (1) points earned during the oral reading for that week and (2) points earned on a comprehension quiz covering the content the children have read during the sessions. The winning team is announced, and the children are reassigned the following week.

READ MORE ABOUT IT

◆ ◆ ◆

Delquadri, J., Greenwood, C. R., Whorton, D., Carta, J., and Hall, R. V. (1986). Classwide peer tutoring. *Exceptional Children*, 52, 535–542.

Topping, Keith, and Ehly, S. (1998). *Peer assisted learning*. Mahwah, NJ: Erlbaum.

Self-Selected Reading

◆　◆　◆

Also known as Drop Everything and Read (DEAR), Uninterrupted Sustained Silent Reading (USSR), and by several other acronyms, self-selected reading is a method of providing students with time during the school day for recreational reading. It provides the opportunity to explore books in a relaxed atmosphere, without the threat of accountability. It also affords a chance to become more fluent. The following guidelines are common in effective programs.

Begin by establishing a policy for acceptable materials. In content classrooms, teachers who might object to allotting instructional time for recreational reading tend to be more receptive to the idea that students might be allowed to select only content-related materials. By assembling a classroom library of trade books and magazines, there will be no shortage of appropriate materials. Library books are also acceptable as long as they relate in some way to the content subject.

In language arts classrooms, there may be greater latitude in the materials students are allowed to select. It is important that they be at an appropriate level of difficulty. The popular Accelerated Reader™ system can be helpful in identifying such books.

SUGGESTIONS FOR A SELF-SELECTED READING SESSION

There is no single way to conduct a self-selected reading session. It may be short or long, regularly scheduled or arranged only as time permits. A few suggestions may help.

◆ *Make sure students select books in advance.* Once the period begins, quiet must prevail. A classroom collection will help since students without something to read can be given a minute or two in which to make a selection.

◆ *Ensure silence.* Other potential interruptions must be discouraged as well. These include talking to one's neighbor, asking questions (even when they concern the reading material!), and sharpening pencils. Violations of this rule are to be met with the termination of self-selected reading for all students. Other punishment, even chastisement, is unnecessary. Culprits soon get the point! Outside distractions should also be discouraged by hanging a sign outside the door: "Do Not Disturb—Reading in Progress."

• *Conduct conferences.* Pat Cunningham suggests that self-selected reading time affords an opportunity to take students aside individually and chat quietly about their reading or their content area learning.

• *Prohibit studying.* Self-selected reading is not a study hall, even though studying often involves books and reading. The idea is to promote reading by giving students a chance to explore the world of books. For this reason, scheduling self-selected reading just before tests is a poor idea. Better times are just after lunch or immediately following recess or physical education.

• *Encourage sharing.* Discussion groups in which children tell about what they've been reading can be a powerful means of building a true community of readers in your classroom.

TEACHING VARIATIONS

Try scheduling self-selected reading on a schoolwide basis. At a given time, everyone reads, including the administration, staff, and visitors. Such a policy underscores the importance of reading—and it certainly assures that the intercom will not be a problem!

Try self-selected reading in content subjects, limiting appropriate materials to novels, nonfiction tradebooks, and magazines that deal with the subject. This approach can encourage wide reading within a content area and allow children to pursue budding interests that may have been piqued in class. A key is to have adequate materials available to make it happen.

READ MORE ABOUT IT
◆ ◆ ◆

Cunningham, Patricia M., and Allington, Richard L. (1999). *Classrooms that work: They can all read and write* (2nd ed.). New York: HarperCollins.

SECTION 3

♦ ♦ ♦

Vocabulary Strategies

Guiding Principles
of Teaching Vocabulary

◆ ◆ ◆

What has research told us about teaching vocabulary? Actually, a great deal is known about how teachers can significantly expand students' word knowledge. Here are some of the most important lessons:

◆ *Preteach key terms to improve comprehension.* This does not mean that every unfamiliar word needs to be introduced before students begin a reading selection, however. Readers are able to tolerate text in which as many as 15% of the words are not fully known.

● *Adopt intensive general vocabulary programs.* It's beneficial to teach new words systematically over a long period of time. Keep in mind, though, that the majority of word meanings are acquired incidentally, through reading and listening. Intensive instruction will never account for more than a small fraction of students' vocabularies.

● *Introduce new words in related clusters.* This advice is true for content area terms and general vocabulary alike. Interconnectedness makes words easier to learn.

● *Employ teaching techniques that stress the connections among related terms.* These include charts, diagrams, and other thematic approaches.

● *Provide more than definitions.* Avoid assigning a weekly list and simply hoping for the best. Students can memorize definitions, to be sure, but their knowledge of terms presented this way is likely to be superficial and short-lived.

● *Tie new words to old knowledge.* Linking the new with the known is the only way that word meanings will be integrated with prior knowledge so that the new words can be used appropriately.

● *Use a combination of definitions and contextual examples.* Doing so demonstrates the deeper meanings of words and models correct and incorrect usage.

● *Provide for brief periodic review.* Occasionally revisiting previously introduced terms for short, intensive review sessions helps to ensure long-term retention.

35

● *Maximize the volume of reading students do.* Nagy has called this "the single most important thing a teacher can do to promote vocabulary growth" (1988, p. 38).

● *Stress the chief tools students need to acquire word meanings as they read.* These are context and structural analysis. Do all you can to ensure that students attempt to apply these skills as they read independently.

● *Be aware of the limitations of definitions.* Formal dictionary definitions can be difficult to understand and even misleading. They are usually insufficient as a means of learning new words.

● *Minimize rote copying of definitions.* Dictionary use is an important skill, but precious time is wasted by having students copy definitions. The tedium involved can be truly numbing as well.

READ MORE ABOUT IT
◆ ◆ ◆

Nagy, William E. (1988). *Teaching vocabulary to improve reading comprehension.* Newark, DE: International Reading Association.

Stahl, Steven A. (1999). *Vocabulary development: From research to practice* (Vol. 2). Cambridge, MA: Brookline Books.

Feature Analysis

◆　◆　◆

Feature analysis, introduced by Johnson and Pearson (1984), is a vocabulary strategy that is useful whenever a cluster of new terms represents members of the same category. This technique makes use of a simple chart. In the upper left-hand corner of the chart, the name of the category is written. The category members are written in the first column. Across the top of the chart, the column headings are various features that each concept might or might not possess. The chart is completed by placing a plus sign (+) in a particular position if the concept in that row has the feature for that column. If not, a zero (0) is used. Some teachers find the letter *s* helpful if a concept *sometimes* has that feature.

The feature analysis chart permits comparisons of any pair of concepts by noting features shared, features possessed by only one of the concepts, and features possessed by neither concept. The chart also facilitates the analysis of each feature by considering which concepts possess it and which do not.

Step 1. Place an empty chart on the board or project it with a transparency. In the upper left-hand corner, place the name of the category. Tell students they will be helping you fill in the chart with some of the words they have been studying.

Step 2. Ask the students to suggest words that are examples of the word you have written in the upper left-hand box. Add additional examples the students do not mention but that you know need to be included in the chart.

Step 3. Write down key features at the head of each of the remaining columns. You are the best judge of these.

Step 4. Together with the students, complete the chart row by row, deciding together whether each category member possesses each of the key features. Discuss the terms as you go.

Step 5. Make comparisons of category members based on the completed chart. Focus on which features they have in common and where they differ.

EXAMPLE

After a teaching unit on the planets, a teacher might construct a chart in order to highlight similarities and differences among the nine planets of our solar system. Teachers might disagree as to which features to include as column headings. There is no formula for choosing them. The following chart is one possibility.

Planets (in order from sun)	Has a moon or moons	Rocky surface	Has rings
Mercury	0	+	0
Venus	0	+	0
Earth	+	+	0
Mars	+	+	0
Jupiter	+	0	0
Saturn	+	0	+
Uranus	+	0	+
Neptune	+	0	+
Pluto	+	+	0

Once the chart has been completed, the teacher might use it to point out interesting facts. For example, only the two innermost planets have no moons, and planets with rocky surfaces do not have rings.

A limitation of feature analysis charts is evident in this example. Whenever two or more concepts have identical patterns of pluses and zeros, there is not enough information to tell them apart. In this case, Saturn, Uranus, and Neptune appear to be identical. One way to differentiate them, if a teacher felt it useful to do so, would be to add columns (new features) that capture differences.

TEACHING VARIATIONS

Feature analysis has an unusually close relationship to formal definitions. In fact, students can actually construct definitions based on the chart. This is done by choosing one of the concepts along the left and stating that it is an example of the category mentioned in the top left box and has or does not have whatever features are indicated. For example, these two definitions come straight from the chart:

Earth = a planet with a moon and a rocky surface but no rings
Venus = a planet with a rocky surface and without moons or rings

These are close to the dictionary definitions, though some of the definitions composed from a feature analysis chart tend to be longer and more awkward. Nevertheless, the two required elements of all good definitions are present: the category and the distinguishing features. Definition construction is an excellent writing activity that can be used to follow up a reading assignment that has been introduced by means of feature analysis.

Another way to use feature analysis charts is to set purposes for reading. Whenever the content is appropriate, the students read a selection with the goal of completing the chart. Of course, the chart would need to be adequately introduced and at least one row filled in by the teacher as an example. This makes an excellent inferential reading activity, one that requires no tedious copying—just pluses and zeros!

Feature analysis is not limited to a particular subject or even to technical terminology in the usual sense. For example, a useful chart involving characters from a short story or novel, analyzed by character traits, is quite possible. Such charts are so useful and versatile that we offer several black-line masters in the following pages to be duplicated as needed. The first two take the form of exercises to familiarize your students with how the charts work.

READ MORE ABOUT IT

◆ ◆ ◆

Johnson, Dale D., and Pearson, P. David. (1984). *Teaching reading vocabulary* (2nd ed.). New York: Holt, Rinehart & Winston.

Pittelman, Susan D., Heimlich, Joan E., Berglund, Roberta L., and French, Michael P. (1991). *Semantic feature analysis: Classroom applications*. Newark, DE: International Reading Association. [Order online at http://www.reading.org, or call 302-731-1600]

Name _____ Teacher _____ Date _____

Write the names of five students in the left column of this chart. Then read the words above each column. Decide whether the words describe each person. Write a plus if the words describe the person or a zero if they do not.

Student	Girl	Brown eyes

From *Help for Struggling Readers* by Michael C. McKenna. Copyright 2002 by The Guilford Press. Permission to photocopy this page is granted to purchasers of this book for personal use only (see copyright page for details).

Name _____ Teacher _____ Date _____

Each word in the left column of this chart is a pet. The words above each column may or may not be true of each pet. Decide whether the words really describe each pet. Write a plus if the words describe the pet or a zero if they do not.

Pets	Fur	Four legs	Lives in a cage	Breathes air
dog				
cat				
bird				
fish				
gerbil				

From *Help for Struggling Readers* by Michael C. McKenna. Copyright 2002 by The Guilford Press. Permission to photocopy this page is granted to purchasers of this book for personal use only (see copyright page for details).

Name _____

From *Help for Struggling Readers* by Michael C. McKenna. Copyright 2002 by The Guilford Press. Permission to photocopy this page is granted to purchasers of this book for personal use only (see copyright page for details).

Name _____

From *Help for Struggling Readers* by Michael C. McKenna. Copyright 2002 by The Guilford Press. Permission to photocopy this page is granted to purchasers of this book for personal use only (see copyright page for details).

Name _____ Teacher _____ Date _____

From *Help for Struggling Readers* by Michael C. McKenna. Copyright 2002 by The Guilford Press. Permission to photocopy this page is granted to purchasers of this book for personal use only (see copyright page for details).

Graphic Organizers

♦ ♦ ♦

A graphic organizer is a diagram showing how key concepts are related. Examples abound in textbooks, though they can also be constructed by teachers and students. Some types of graphic organizers include:

♦ Time lines
♦ Tree diagrams
♦ Venn diagrams
♦ Labeled pictures
♦ Graphs
♦ Sociograms
♦ Semantic maps and webs

Each of these types has been used to introduce technical terms in clusters, showing students how the terms are related to one another. This approach does not mean that the definitions do not need to be taught. Rather, graphic organizers provide a means of going beyond the definitions, allowing students to grasp interrelationships among concepts.

There are many advantages to graphic organizers:

♦ They help kids "see" abstract content.
♦ There is little to "read."
♦ They are easy to construct and discuss.
♦ They allow technical terms to be taught in clusters.
♦ They provide a way to organize content learning for better recall and understanding.
♦ Their use is validated by extensive research with varied populations.

Several simple steps should help you construct a good graphic organizer:

1. Make a list of key terms.
2. Identify clusters of closely related terms within the list.
3. Determine how the words in each cluster are related.
4. Arrange the words in each cluster into a diagram.

(Note that several graphic organizers may come from your original list!)
Here are some tips for using graphic organizers effectively.

1. Decide when to introduce the organizer. In most cases it will work best toward the end of a chapter or unit, as a way of pulling content together. When students have adequate background knowledge, however, an organizer might be used effectively prior to assigned reading.
2. Make sure you introduce an organizer with plenty of discussion and explanation.
3. If you are constructing an organizer, look for ways of including some terms that are already familiar to students. Doing so will help them associate new learning with previous content.
4. Encourage students to construct their own organizers. This will become feasible after you have exposed students to a variety of organizers over time. Begin by asking them to complete partially constructed organizers, and move to situations in which students develop their own, given only a list of terms.
5. Couple organizers with reading guides. Once students have caught on to how graphic organizers work, they can be expected to complete or construct them during guided reading of nonfiction. These two proven strategies–graphic organizers and reading guides—work well in combination!

The following pages contain examples of various kinds of graphic organizers, reprinted from McKenna and Robinson (2002).*

*Copyright 2002 by Addison Wesley/Longman. Reprinted by permission.

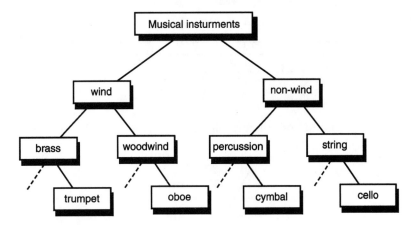

Graphic organizer: Tree diagram for musical instruments.

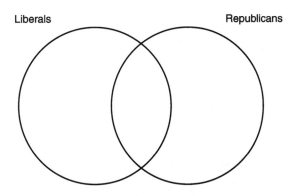

Graphic organizer: Venn diagram for liberals and Republicans.

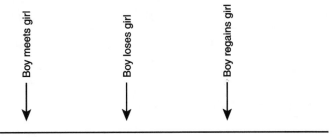

Graphic organizer: Time line without specific dates.

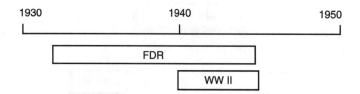

Graphic organizer: Time line for World War II.

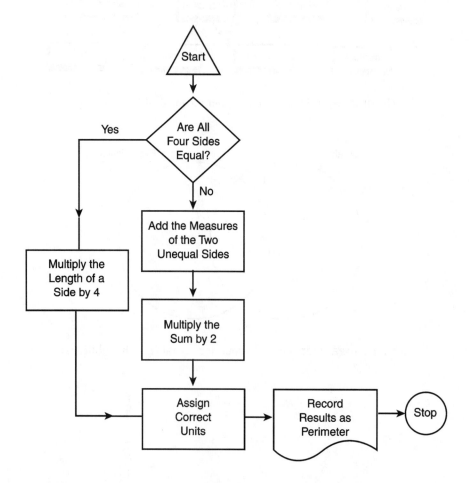

Graphic organizer: Flowchart for finding the perimeter of a rectangle.

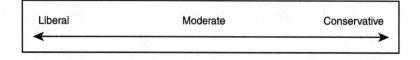

Graphic organizer: Continuum showing political orientations.

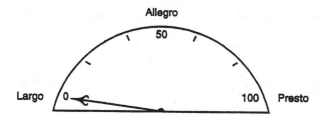

Graphic organizer: A musical "speedometer" (some elements omitted).

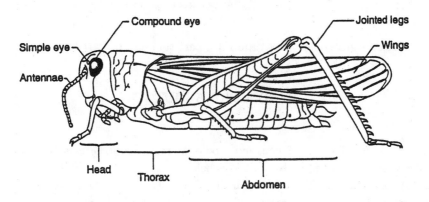

Graphic organizer: Labeled picture for parts of an insect.

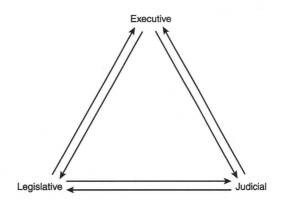

Graphic organizer: Sociogram for checks and balances among the three branches of government.

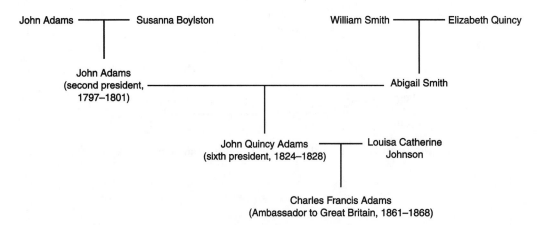

An American family tree: Part time line, part sociogram, part tree diagram!

READ MORE ABOUT IT

◆ ◆ ◆

Bromley, Karen, Irwin-De Vitis, Linda, and Modlo, Marcia. (1995). *Graphic organizers: Visual strategies for active learning.* New York: Scholastic.

McKenna, Michael C., and Robinson, Richard D. (2002). *Teaching through text: A content literacy approach to content area reading* (3rd ed.). New York: Longman. [See Chapter 6]

Name _____

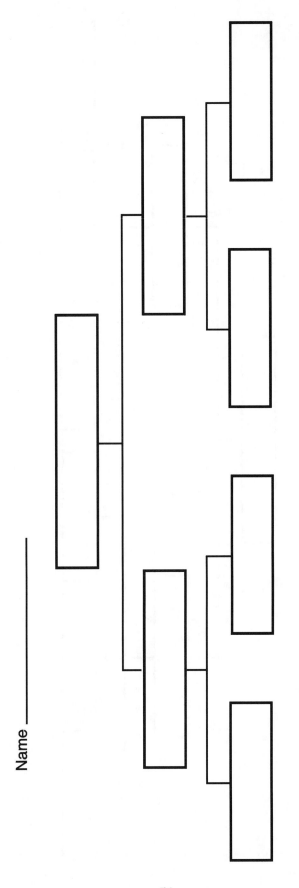

From *Help for Struggling Readers* by Michael C. McKenna. Copyright 2002 by The Guilford Press. Permission to photocopy this page is granted to purchasers of this book for personal use only (see copyright page for details).

Name _____

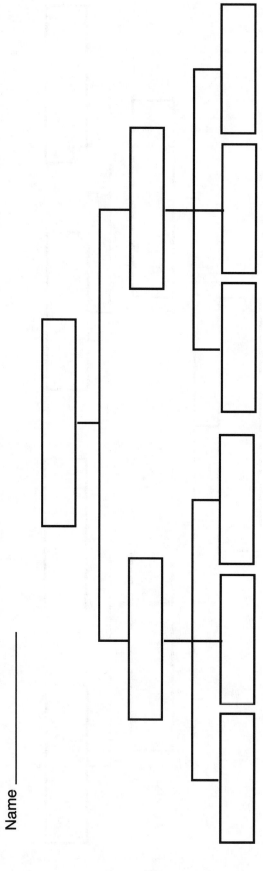

From *Help for Struggling Readers* by Michael C. McKenna. Copyright 2002 by The Guilford Press. Permission to photocopy this page is granted to purchasers of this book for personal use only (see copyright page for details).

Name _____

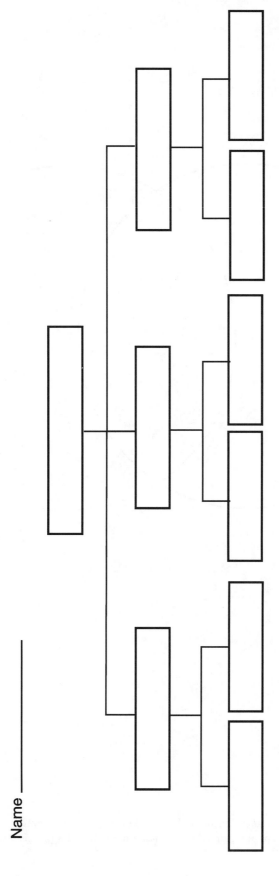

From *Help for Struggling Readers* by Michael C. McKenna. Copyright 2002 by The Guilford Press. Permission to photocopy this page is granted to purchasers of this book for personal use only (see copyright page for details).

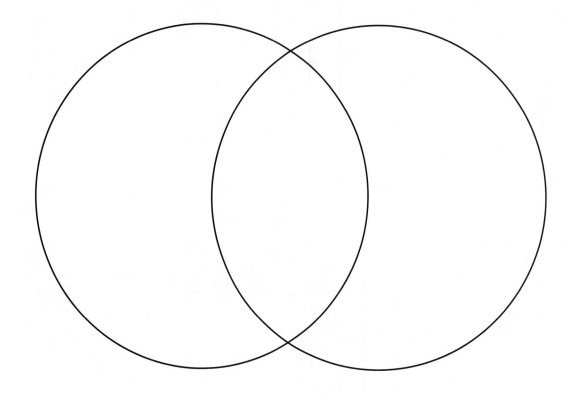

From *Help for Struggling Readers* by Michael C. McKenna. Copyright 2002 by The Guilford Press. Permission to photocopy this page is granted to purchasers of this book for personal use only (see copyright page for details).

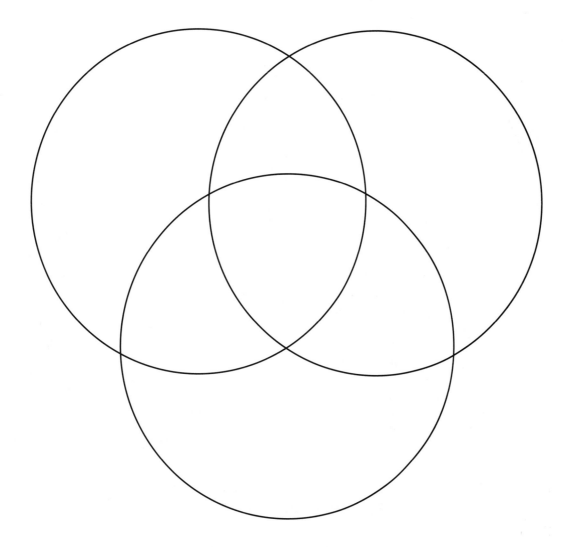

From *Help for Struggling Readers* by Michael C. McKenna. Copyright 2002 by The Guilford Press. Permission to photocopy this page is granted to purchasers of this book for personal use only (see copyright page for details).

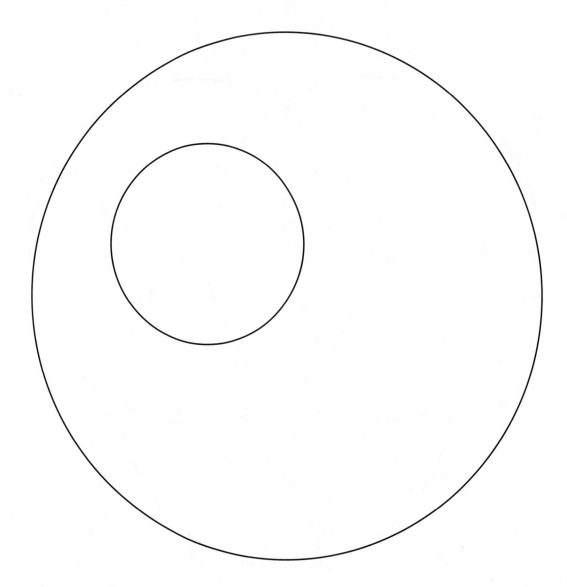

From *Help for Struggling Readers* by Michael C. McKenna. Copyright 2002 by The Guilford Press. Permission to photocopy this page is granted to purchasers of this book for personal use only (see copyright page for details).

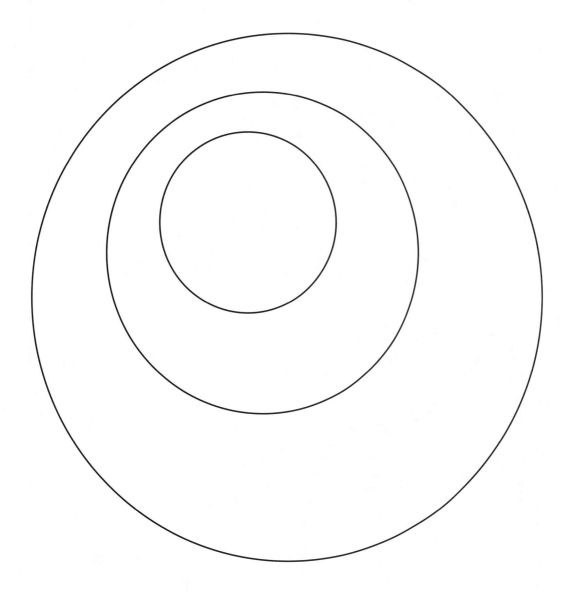

From *Help for Struggling Readers* by Michael C. McKenna. Copyright 2002 by The Guilford Press. Permission to photocopy this page is granted to purchasers of this book for personal use only (see copyright page for details).

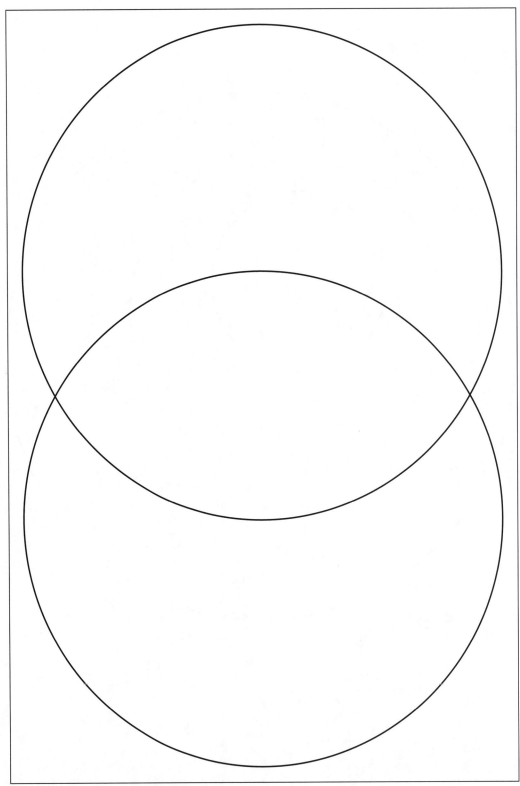

From *Help for Struggling Readers* by Michael C. McKenna. Copyright 2002 by The Guilford Press. Permission to photocopy this page is granted to purchasers of this book for personal use only (see copyright page for details).

Semantic Maps

◆ ◆ ◆

A semantic map is a freewheeling diagram with a key concept at the center and related concepts placed at the ends of radiating spokes. It is sometimes called a "semantic web" or "spider" diagram. It is an easy diagram to make, and students can be engaged in suggesting words to be included in the map. Semantic maps derive their instructional power by stressing the connections among word meanings. They help students organize what they know, making it both more meaningful and more memorable.

Semantic mapping can be used either before or after reading—or both! If used beforehand, the technique activates (and helps the teacher assess) students' prior knowledge of the topic. If used afterward, it helps students reorganize the new words they have learned. Heimlich and Pittelman's description of the approach (1986) can be summarized in these steps:

Step 1. Present a central concept and have students brainstorm words that are related to that concept. List these on the board.

Step 2. Add words that you know to be important but that students do not mention.

Step 3. Quickly supply working definitions of these terms.

Step 4. Together with the children, develop the semantic map, starting with the central concept. Make public decisions about which words belong on which spokes.

Step 5. Make sure that a key concept anchors the end of each spoke. Draw a box or oval around it.

Step 6. If semantic mapping is used prior to reading, leave a spoke or two blank so that additional words can be added later.

Stahl's (1999) summary of research into the effectiveness of semantic mapping led to the following conclusions:

◆ Semantic mapping can improve students' word knowledge.
◆ Semantic mapping can improve students' comprehension of passages containing the words included in the map.

♦ Class discussion and active group map-building are far more effective than simply providing ready-made semantic maps.

♦ Semantic mapping seems to be especially effective with the poorest readers.

EXAMPLE

Here is an example of a finished product that follows the steps outlined above. The key concept (the American Revolution) is broad enough to touch on many related concepts, some of which are obviously quite familiar. Note how six important terms (Declaration of Independence, Great Britain, generals, battles, causes, and outcomes) anchor the spokes. These words were suggested by the teacher in an effort to organize the list brainstormed by the students. Students' words are italicized.

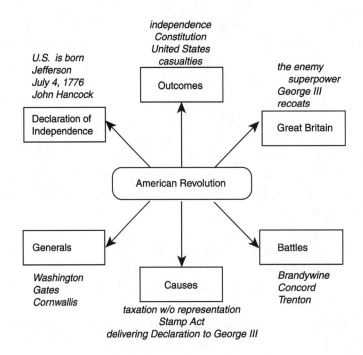

independence
Constitution
United States
casualties

Outcomes

U.S. is born
Jefferson
July 4, 1776
John Hancock

Declaration of Independence

the enemy
superpower
George III
recoats

Great Britain

American Revolution

Generals

Washington
Gates
Cornwallis

Causes

taxation w/o representation
Stamp Act
delivering Declaration to George III

Battles

Brandywine
Concord
Trenton

A blank reproducible, sometimes called a "spider diagram," appears on page 61. Try using it as a transparency, a student handout, or both!

READ MORE ABOUT IT
♦ ♦ ♦

Heimlich, Joan E., and Pittelman, Susan D. (1986). *Semantic mapping: Classroom applications.* Newark, DE: International Reading Association.

Stahl, Steven A. (1999). *Vocabulary development: From research to practice* (Vol. 2). Cambridge, MA: Brookline Books.

Name _____

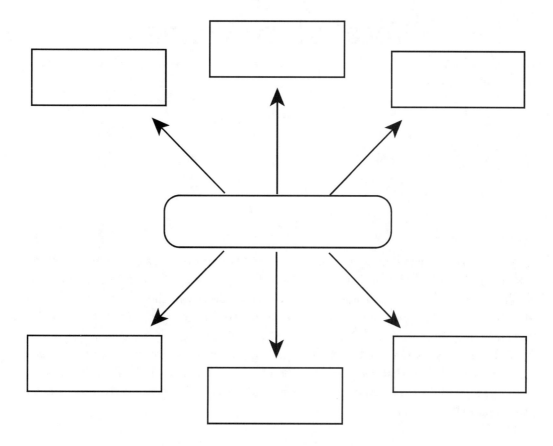

From *Help for Struggling Readers* by Michael C. McKenna. Copyright 2002 by The Guilford Press. Permission to photocopy this page is granted to purchasers of this book for personal use only (see copyright page for details).

Vocabulary Venns

◆ ◆ ◆

Venn diagrams can be very useful in explaining the differences between two closely related words, like near synonyms. Here is a quick way of using Venns to accomplish this goal. The approach assumes that you have already introduced the meanings of the two words. The diagram simply helps students master important distinctions between them.

Through discussion, ask the students to suggest what qualities the two words have in common and also what each has that the other lacks. A two-circle Venn diagram allows these qualities to be categorized easily and visually. The example below is taken from Stahl (1999, p. 44).*

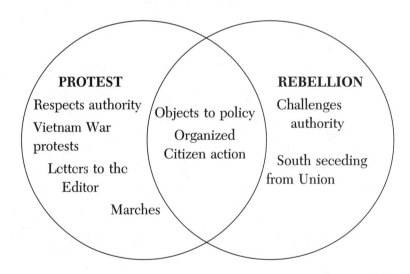

PROTEST

Respects authority

Vietnam War protests

Letters to the Editor

Marches

Objects to policy
Organized
Citizen action

REBELLION

Challenges authority

South seceding from Union

*Copyright 1999 by Brookline Books. Reprinted by permission.

This example shows how the two key words can be central to understanding content units in science, social studies, and other subjects. Pairs of related terms can be routinely compared and contrasted in this way. Consider these pairs:

state versus colony
band versus orchestra
monocot versus dicot
bacteria versus viruses
reptile versus amphibian

READ MORE ABOUT IT
◆ ◆ ◆

Stahl, Steven A. (1999). *Vocabulary development: From research to practice* (Vol. 2). Cambridge, MA: Brookline Books.

Semantic Scales

♦ ♦ ♦

A semantic scale uses the simplest of diagrams—a straight line—to express relation-ships among words that vary in degree. The scale is anchored at each end by a word familiar to the students. The two words at either end of the scale are antonyms. New words are then written on the scale after they are introduced and discussed. The following example uses the words *hot* and *cold* to create a scale that relates to heat:

hot ← → cold

As the students study words that convey a sense of temperature, they are placed on the scale at appropriate places.

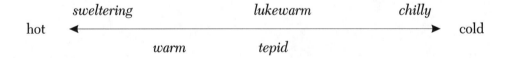

There may be disagreements among students about the best place to put a word. This is part of a healthy discussion!

The main advantage of semantic scales is that they allow new words to be rein-forced in related clusters. This aids retention and deepens understanding of word meanings. They also invite active engagement as students apply their knowledge of word meanings. Cooperative group processing can be very useful in creating semantic scales.

CONNOTATIONS

Another use of semantic scales is to discuss how words can convey a positive or negative message even though their formal meanings are very nearly the same. Here's an example of how synonyms for *thin* can be placed along a scale from negative to positive connotations. This approach is a simple and effective activity for deepening students' word knowledge after the words have been studied.

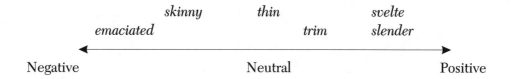

Negative   Neutral   Positive

List–Group–Label

◆ ◆ ◆

Hilda Taba's List–Group–Label is a vocabulary strategy that is especially useful toward the end of a content unit. It causes students to actively reorganize what they have learned, making it easier to understand and remember.

Step 1. Begin by suggesting to the class a major topic they have been studying. In the List stage, ask the students to brainstorm all the words they have learned in association with the topic. Record these words on the board or transparency until 25 or 30 have been accumulated.

Step 2. In the Group stage, have the students work together to rearrange the words into categories. They needn't be concerned with the exact nature of the categories at this point. Their goal is simply to group words that have some connection.

Step 3. Finally, in the Label stage, each category of words is given an appropriate designation. Occasionally some of the words may be left over without clear-cut category membership. Encourage students not to worry about these cases but to suggest instead category labels for each leftover term.

List–Group–Label has several notable strengths. It focuses on the interrelationships that exist among technical vocabulary words. It provides an environment for actively engaging students with the content (and is especially well suited to collaborative activities). It provides a good method of linking the new with the familiar.

EXAMPLE

A class has nearly completed its study of rocks. The teacher begins by asking class members to name any of the terms they've studied. The board (or transparency) is soon filled with words like these

metamorphic	seismic	obsidian	limestone
granite	sandstone	core	flint
crust	igneous	sedimentary	basalt
mantle	shale	quartz	gypsum

With the teacher's help, the students then attempt to arrange the words into small groupings. Part of the board space or transparency might be reserved in order to recopy the words into these groupings.

metamorphic	obsidian	crust	seismic
igneous	granite	mantle	
sedimentary	sandstone	core	
	quartz		
	shale		
	limestone		
	basalt		
	flint		
	gypsum		

The word *seismic* does not seem to fit with any of the other words, so it is left by itself as a group of one. Next, the students suggest labels for each of the groupings.

Types of rocks	Minerals	Parts of the earth	Vibrations in the earth
metamorphic	obsidian	crust	seismic
igneous	granite	mantle	
sedimentary	sandstone	core	
	quartz		
	shale		
	limestone		
	basalt		
	flint		
	gypsum		

A discussion of how the labels fit and whether any additional terms can be added to any of the groups should follow.

READ MORE ABOUT IT

◆ ◆ ◆

McKenna, Michael C., and Robinson, Richard D. (2001). *Teaching through text: A content literacy approach to content area reading* (3rd ed.). New York: Longman.

Tierney, Robert J., and Readence, John E. (2000). *Reading strategies and practices: A compendium* (5th ed.). Boston: Allyn & Bacon.

Concept Sorts

◆ ◆ ◆

Concept sorts are activities that require students to place words into categories based not on physical features (as in phonics word sorts) but on the meanings they represent. Of course, the word meanings must be related in some way, making such sorts ideal for content area units.

Used as a prereading activity, a concept sort can provide information about how much students already know about a topic. They can also be used to set purposes for later reading and study. Donald Bear and his colleagues (2000) suggest playing a game called "Guess My Category." The teacher writes several words on the board while introducing a unit. As an example, here are a few related concepts from your own profession:

principal
school secretary
classroom teacher
reading specialist
superintendent
curriculum director
assistant principal
special education teacher
school bus driver
school custodian

One of the students' tasks as they read and study is to infer a category label linking the concepts. The list is revisited later as the unit is reviewed and students are asked to provide a label. (What label would you give to the list above?)

Used as a postreading activity, a concept sort causes students to think logically about word meanings. It also strengthens knowledge about important connections among words. A concept sort is similar to List–Group–Label in that students end up with two or more categorized word lists. Unlike List–Group–Label, however, the teacher supplies the initial list of words.

Like phonics word sorts, concept sorts can be open or closed (Gillet and Kita, 1979). In open word sorts, the categories are not supplied in advance by the teacher. The students must look within the list for features shared by two or more words. Consider again the list above. How might you group some of these words? You would need to use your prior knowledge of these occupations to discern commonalities. It would be easier, of course, to begin not only with the list but with a set of categories. If the following headings were arranged on the board at the beginning, the task would become far more straightforward:

Administrators	Teachers	Classified staff
principal	classroom teacher	school secretary
superintendent	reading specialist	school bus driver
curriculum director	special education teacher	school custodian
assistant principal		

The task has now become a closed word sort. Closed sorts are a good starting point for introducing students to the process of categorization. They provide a good foundation both for open sorts and for List–Group–Label, which is really a type of open sort. Remember that open sorts are just that—your students may categorize some of the words along unpredictable lines. For example, you might have formed two categories for the list above: persons with and without teaching certificates.

READ MORE ABOUT IT

♦ ♦ ♦

Bear, Donald R., Invernizzi, Marcia, Templeton, Shane, and Johnston, Francine. (2000). *Words their way: Word study for phonics, vocabulary, and spelling instruction* (2nd ed.). Upper Saddle River, NJ: Prentice Hall.

Gillet, J., and Kita, M. J. (1979). Words, kids, and categories. *The Reading Teacher, 32,* 538–542.

Vocabulary Clusters

◆ ◆ ◆

It's hard to learn new words when their meanings are not related. A random list must be learned one word at a time, and the work is both difficult and tedious. This is because word meanings are not stored in this fashion but in elaborate connections with one another. And, as Stahl puts it, "If words are stored in categories, then it makes sense to teach them that way" (1999, p. 40). When words are grouped on the basis of a theme, or linking concept, they are much easier to learn. Relationships among the new terms assist the learner in appreciating their precise meanings.

Introducing terms in clusters and creating activities that capitalize on what they have in common increases the effectiveness of general vocabulary instruction. In content subjects, of course, it is easy to think of themes that link new terms; for example:

polygons: square, rhombus, quadrilateral, pentagon, etc.
governments: democracy, dictatorship, oligarchy, monarchy, etc.

Teaching techniques such as semantic feature analysis charts and graphic organizers are useful in explaining the relationships among such terms. These same techniques can sometimes be used in teaching general vocabulary arranged in clusters. Sometimes, however, more creative methods are called for.

The most important requirement is that you think in terms of *themes*. The words will then nearly suggest themselves, and a short unit can be developed quickly. In listing words related to a theme, do not hesitate to include words you're certain the children already know. This helps them link the new with the known.

At the end of this chapter, sample vocabulary clusters are presented along with an idea or two for teaching them. The words are deliberately limited to terms rarely taught in content area classes.

READ MORE ABOUT IT

◆ ◆ ◆

Beck, Isabel L., Perfetti, Charles A., & McKeown, Margaret G. (1982). Effects of long-term vocabulary instruction on lexical access and reading comprehension. *Journal of Educational Psychology, 74,* 506–521.

Marzano, Robert J., and Marzano, Jana S. (1988). *A cluster approach to elementary vocabulary instruction* (Reading AIDS Series). Newark, DE: International Reading Association.

Stahl, Steven A. (1999). *Vocabulary development: From research to practice* (Vol. 2). Cambridge, MA: Brookline Books.

OFF-COLOR WORDS

mauve	light purple
taupe	dark brownish-gray
teal	dark greenish-blue
ocher	reddish brown
aqua	light blue-green
saffron	orange-yellow
beige	tan
puce	brownish purple
turquoise	slightly greenish blue

Teaching Tip: Bring in pictures showing each shade. Then ask students to bring pictured examples. Use them to construct a poster.

MOODS

pensive	thoughtful
depressed	sad
energetic	full of energy
elated	very happy
argumentative	tending to argue
bellicose	quarrelsome or hostile
lighthearted	not serious
sullen	gloomy, refusing to talk

Teaching Tip: Ask students to act out each mood or to think of fictional characters they associate with a mood.

Teaching Tip: Consider pairs of mood words in combination. For example, could a person be elated and lighthearted at the same time? Depressed and bellicose?

HOT, COLD, and IN-BETWEEN

torrid	tepid	frosty
sultry	lukewarm	numbing
sweltering	mild	frigid
scorching		icy
blazing		wintry

Teaching Tip: Use a semantic scale to place these words in perspective.

Teaching Tip: Use the weather each day to quickly revisit the terms.

ROADWAYS

avenue	a street often lined with trees, often at right angles to "streets"
thoroughfare	a main road with much traffic
boulevard	a broad street, often lined with trees
lane	a narrow road or walkway, often in the country
alley	a narrow street located behind houses or other buildings
superhighway	same as interstate highway
turnpike	any road you must pay to use

Teaching Tip: Ask students to find streets of each kind in their neighborhood or on a map.

PERSONALITY TRAITS

introverted	avoiding others
extraverted	enjoying the company of others
even-tempered	seldom mad
moody	changing moods quickly and without real cause
quick-tempered	easily angered
friendly	warm, sociable
cooperative	willing to work with others
optimistic	looking on the bright side, expecting the best
pessimistic	looking on the gloomy side, expecting the worst
abrasive	rude, unable to get along well with others

Teaching Tip: Ask students to describe an incident where one of these traits became obvious in someone.

FRENCH DESSERTS

torte	a rich cake, often with chopped nuts
parfait	dessert made of rich cream and other ingredients and served in a tall, slender, short-stemmed glass
crème brulee	cream dessert served in a flat dish and slightly scorched on the surface
éclair	a small, oblong pasty shell filled with custard or whipped cream
mousse	a light, chilled dessert made from egg whites, whipped cream, and sometimes fruit
nonpareil	a chocolate drop covered with tiny balls of sugar

Teaching Tip: Bring in one or more of these to school for sampling by students. Give each child a plastic spoon to avoid spreading germs.

COLLECTIVE NOUNS

pride	lions
school	fish
herd	cattle (etc.)
gaggle	geese
flock	sheep (etc.)
fleet	ships
cluster	grapes (etc.)
bouquet	flowers
litter	puppies
swarm	bees

Teaching Tip: There are many others. Ask students to add to the list.

BRITISH WORDS

lorry	truck
lift	elevator
flat	apartment
bonnet	hood of a car
boot	trunk of a car
windscreen	windshield of a car
water closet	bathroom (often abbreviated W.C.)
loo	bathroom (slang)
crisps	potato chips
headmaster	principal
petrol	gasoline
spanner	monkey wrench
biscuit	a crisp, flat cookie

Teaching Tip: Have the students write ordinary sentences containing two or more British terms.

VOICES

shrill	high-pitched and irritating
grating	harsh, annoying
raspy	rough-sounding
sonorous	full, deep, and rich in sound
mellifluous	sweet, smooth and honeylike
squeaky	high-pitched and uneven; Mickey Mouse-like
nasal	caused by too much air passing through the nose

Teaching Tip: Ask students to identify famous persons with voices of each type. Think of a few yourself in advance.

NEAT MEAT WE EAT

beef	comes from a	cow
pork	comes from a	pig
mutton	comes from a	sheep (adult)
venison	comes from a	deer
veal	comes from a	calf

Teaching Tip: Cook up a sampler of a few types and bring it to class.

TYPES OF DISEASES

chronic	persistent, not going away
congenital	existing from birth
hereditary	inherited from parents or ancestors
terminal	leading to death
contagious	spread from person to person
infectious	resulting from and spread by infection

Teaching Tip: Suggest one or two diseases of each type and ask students to suggest others.

WHERE PEOPLE LIVE

metropolis	large city
suburb	town on the edge of a large city
slum	low-income area of a city
hamlet	very small town
inner city	residential section of city
subdivision	suburban housing development

Teaching Tip: Use a state or local map to identify examples.

FABULOUS FABRICS

suede	corduroy	damask
linen	terry cloth	silk
satin	denim	tweed
flannel	polyester	velvet

Teaching Tip: The obvious approach is to assemble swatches of these materials. Garments might also be brought to class.

BIRTHSTONES

garnet	January, dark red
amethyst	February, purple
bloodstone	March, dark green with red spots
diamond	April
emerald	May, green
pearl	June, gray-white
ruby	July, red
sardonyx	August, white and orange-red layers
sapphire	September, deep blue
opal	October, translucent, multicolored
topaz	November, pale blue
turquoise	December, bright blue

Teaching Tip: Use a birthstone chart to introduce the stones. Some students may have birthstone rings to share.

HE SAID, SHE SAID

Alternative ways of saying "said" are useful to writers and readers alike. Students need to appreciate the sometimes subtle differences among them. Using the past tense works best because that's the form in which these words most often appear. Here is a good list to permanently post for quick reference, but add to it slowly, when appropriate examples come up.

announced	called	laughed	responded	snarled
answered	declared	mumbled	retorted	snickered
asserted	exclaimed	proclaimed	screamed	stated
bellowed	gushed	rejoined	shot back	suggested
breathed	hinted	remarked	shouted	whispered

Teaching Tip: Write a sentence context on the board, replacing the word for *said* with a blank. Together, try out various words in the blank to see if they work. For example: "Get out of here!" the angry man _____.

Teaching Tip: When reviewing a fiction selection, pause occasionally to ask if a word on the list might work in a particular context.

Teaching Tip: Ask kids to find additional words from the books they're reading. Add them to your list.

FEARFUL WORDS

Capitalize on kids' natural fascination with phobias
by introducing these:

acrophobia	fear of heights
agoraphobia	fear of open spaces
arachniphobia	fear of spiders
claustrophobia	fear of enclosed places
homophobia	fear of homosexuals
xenophobia	fear of foreigners

Teaching Tip: Create new phobias by coining words. For example, a fear of birds would
be ornithophobia, a fear of light photophobia, etc. These words may not
be in the dictionary, but they are legitimate coinages. Kids too can use
word elements to coin their own new fears.

Want more? A lengthy listing of phobias can be found at http://phobialist.com.

WORDS FOR LOVERS

These words all end in *phile*, meaning one who loves:

Anglophile	one who loves England
bibliophile	one who loves books
Francophile	one who loves France

Teaching Tip: Have kids create their own "love words" by using roots or real words
with the -phile suffix. Examples:

gynophile	one who loves women
Bobophile	one who loves Bob

HATS

Types of hats form an engaging word cluster that is ideally
introduced with pictures. Pen-and-ink drawings of most or
all of these can be located in many dictionaries.

beret	glengarry	turban
biretta	helmet	wimple
bonnet	miter	yarmulke
bowler	Panama	tophat
busby	shako	fez
derby	sombrero	fedora
tam-o'-shanter		

Silly Questions

♦ ♦ ♦

An excellent way of deepening word knowledge is to ask what Isabel Beck and her colleagues call "silly questions." These are merely questions that connect two words in interesting ways. For example, let's say a class is reviewing the following general vocabulary words:

accountant
virtuoso
rival
philanthropist
reluctant
scrutinize

Here are some silly questions that might be constructed from this list of vocabulary words. If we pair up nouns, we might have:

"Can an accountant be a philanthropist?"
"Can a virtuoso be a rival?"

We can also pair a noun and an adjective:

"Can a virtuoso be reluctant?"

or a noun and a verb:

"Can an accountant scrutinize something?"

Students need to explain their answers to silly questions and not merely respond "yes" or "no." Their explanations will reveal much about how well they understand the word meanings, and they can form the basis of an interesting, fast-paced discussion.

TEACHING VARIATIONS

Once students catch on to how Silly Questions operate, have them work in pairs or small teams to form their own Silly Questions. Of course, they must first think through appropriate answers before asking their questions of the class.

Keep in mind that the sample list of six words presented above consists of *randomly selected* words with little or no semantic connection. Imagine how well Silly Questions would work if the words were connected through a theme!

Finally, Beck and her colleagues (1982) actually embedded Silly Questions in a 5-day instructional strategy designed to encourage active processing of word meanings. This structure should be useful in grounding a general vocabulary program at almost any grade, but it's likely that Silly Questions will work in many contexts.

Day 1 Introduce words and definitions. Discuss how each word is used in context, being sure to include examples and nonexamples.

Day 2 Review the definitions. Possibly provide students with a list of sentences, each containing a blank. Students must complete the sentences with words from the new vocabulary list. Conduct a "Word Wizard" activity, in which students try to locate words in selected text. (They can accumulate points toward becoming a "Word Wizard.")

Day 3 Provide another homemade worksheet. Conduct a "Ready, Set, Go" activity. Pairs of students try to match words and definitions in the shortest time. Repeat the "Word Wizard" activity.

Day 4 Repeat the "Ready, Set, Go" activity. Repeat the "Word Wizard" activity. Ask silly questions.

Day 5 Give posttest.

This approach led not only to improved word knowledge (compared with providing definitions only) but also to improved comprehension of materials that contained the new words.

READ MORE ABOUT IT

◆ ◆ ◆

Beck, Isabel L., Perfetti, Charles A., and McKeown, Margaret G. (1982). Effects of long-term vocabulary instruction on lexical access and reading comprehension. *Journal of Educational Psychology, 74*, 506–521.

Stahl, Steven A. (1999). *Vocabulary development: From reading research to practice* (Vol. 2). Cambridge, MA: Brookline Books.

Possible Sentences

◆ ◆ ◆

The "possible sentences" technique, developed by Dave and Sharon Moore (1986), is excellent for content units. It stresses clusters of related terms and the *relationships among terms*. Stahl and Kapinus (1991) found that possible sentences improved both vocabulary knowledge and comprehension of material containing targeted words. In fact, it proved more powerful than another very effective approach, semantic mapping. The procedure is quite simple:

- ◆ Choose 6 to 8 unfamiliar words from the new unit.
- ◆ Choose an additional 4 to 6 words likely to be familiar.
- ◆ Put these 10 to 12 words on the board.
- ◆ Provide short definitions, drawing on student knowledge wherever possible.
- ◆ Ask students to think of sentences that use at least two of the words and that express ideas they think they may discover when they read.
- ◆ Write these sentences on the board as the students dictate them.
- ◆ Include both right and wrong guesses.
- ◆ Make sure every word is used in at least one sentence.
- ◆ When the students are finished providing sentences, ask them to read the material.
- ◆ Afterward, discuss the sentences on the board, noting whether each could be true, based now on the reading.
- ◆ If a sentence is true, leave it alone. If it is not, discuss how to modify it to make it true.

EXAMPLE

A middle grades teacher was about to begin a unit on weather. She selected seven bold-faced terms that were introduced in the textbook chapter. These she wrote on the board:

climate
weather
front
isobar
humidity
barometer
meteorology

To these terms she added five more that she felt certain would be somewhat familiar to her sixth-grade students:

hurricane
tornado
sleet
hail
precipitation

Here are three of the sentences generated by the students on the basis of the combined 12-word list. Remember that they were required to use at least two of the terms in each of the sentences they suggested.

   ♦ A barometer is used to measure isobars.
   ♦ Sleet comes in front of a hurricane.
   ♦ Hail is one kind of precipitation.

Note that the third sentence is correct, though it contains none of the new words. The teacher might have begun with two lists (of seven and five words) and required that at least one word in every sentence come from the new list.

READ MORE ABOUT IT
♦ ♦ ♦

Moore, David W., and Moore, Sharon A. (1986). Possible sentences. In E. K. Dishner, T. W. Bean, J. E. Readence, and D. W. Moore (Eds.), *Reading in the content areas: Improving classroom instruction* (2nd ed., pp. 174–179). Dubuque, IA: Kendall/Hunt.

Stahl, Steven A. (1999). *Vocabulary development: From research to practice* (Vol. 2). Cambridge, MA: Brookline Books.

Stahl, Steven A., and Kapinus, Barbara A. (1991). Possible sentences: Predicting word meanings to teach content area vocabulary. *The Reading Teacher, 45,* 36–45.

Tierney, Robert J., and Readence, John E. (2000). *Reading strategies and practices: A compendium* (5th ed.). Boston: Allyn & Bacon.

SECTION 4

◆ ◆ ◆

Comprehension Lesson Formats

Guiding Principles of Teaching Reading Comprehension

◆ ◆ ◆

What has research told us about teaching comprehension? Actually, so much is known that it may seem a little presumptuous to reduce it to a few principles. Nonetheless, it is useful to consider a few of the main findings and to make sure that our teaching strategies embody them. Here are some of the most important lessons:

♦ *Be mindful of the difference between improving general comprehension ability and improving comprehension of a specific selection.* For example, a science teacher may be more concerned with students' comprehending a textbook chapter than with developing their overall comprehension ability. These are different goals, to be sure, though many teaching strategies will lead to both.

● *Preteach key terms to improve comprehension.* Is this a comprehension or a vocabulary principle? Both! We revisit it here as a reminder that important terms should be introduced prior to reading in order to assist comprehension. Even if some of the terms are already familiar to the students, introducing them serves to activate prior knowledge.

● *Build background thoroughly before your students read.* Preteaching key terms is one way, but you will need to find additional ways as well. Providing pictures, diagrams, audiovisuals, factual information, demonstrations, physical props, and discussions of personal experiences your students may have had are just a few possibilities. Remember: It is almost impossible to underestimate the background of some of your struggling readers.

● *Make sure your students' attention is focused as they read.* Providing students with specific purposes for reading will improve comprehension. For example, you may decide to pose questions or provide charts or diagrams to be completed. You may instead ask students to form their own hypotheses or to decide what they themselves wish to learn. There are few restrictions on effective purpose-setting activities.

• *Use activities that cause students to transform information.* By asking students to use the information they find in sentences and paragraphs to complete charts, build diagrams, write summaries, or engage in similar tasks, they must process and understand what they read. This leads to real comprehension.

• *Be cautious about subskill approaches.* Skill-by-skill programs, such as those embodied in a basal reader series, can be useful for organizing instruction, but there is a danger that they can dominate your program and lead to a complacent reliance on worksheets or computerized activities to get the job done.

• *Model comprehension strategies.* Many struggling readers need to be shown how to apply effective strategies. Teachers can model these in class sessions in many ways. A few of these include using think-alouds during discussions, completing reading guides on transparencies, and clustering questions to demonstrate how to answer higher-level questions.

• *Find ways to integrate writing and reading.* Research underscores the important link between these processes. Reading and writing may seem like opposites, but both are *constructive* actions, used by literate people to build meaning. Appropriate activities can involve writing *during* reading (e.g., completing reading guides) or *after* reading (e.g., writing summaries or personal responses).

• *Aim for higher levels of comprehension.* The natural tendency to ask mostly literal-level questions must be resisted. Such questions have their place, to be sure, but unless inferences and critical judgments are included in classroom activities, comprehension may be superficial and inadequate.

READ MORE ABOUT IT

◆ ◆ ◆

Nagy, William E. (1988). *Teaching vocabulary to improve reading comprehension.* Newark, DE: International Reading Association.

Readence, John E., Moore, David W., and Rickelman, Robert J. (2000). *Prereading activities for content area reading and learning* (3rd ed.). Newark, DE: International Reading Association.

Directed Reading Activity

◆ ◆ ◆

The Directed Reading Activity (DRA) is perhaps the oldest systematic method for introducing a reading selection and following it with meaningful activities. Its steps are simple to follow and allow ample room for creative planning.

Step 1. Develop readiness for the reading selection. Try to anticipate deficiencies in prior knowledge of the content and then shore them up by introducing vocabulary, providing factual information, offering visual aids, etc.

Step 2. Set purposes for reading. Such purposes might include reading to answer specific questions, to complete a chart, to reach a conclusion, draw a picture, complete a reading guide, or test a hypothesis. Combinations of these approaches are often possible.

Step 3. Allow students to read the selection. This should be an active process since students now have specific purposes on which to focus while they read.

Step 4. Lead a discussion of the reading selection. The framework of this discussion will be the purpose setting of Step 2, but additional questions are a natural extension.

Step 5. Provide extension or reinforcement activities. These can take many forms and could focus on word recognition, comprehension, or personal responses to content.

The DRA is an extraordinarily flexible lesson format. It can be used with fiction or nonfiction, and the time devoted to each step can be adjusted as appropriate. Some teachers believe that the DRA is too teacher centered, though others view this characteristic as a plus.

READ MORE ABOUT IT

◆ ◆ ◆

Tierney, Robert J., and Readence, John E. (2000). *Reading strategies and practices: A compendium* (5th ed.). Boston: Allyn & Bacon.

Directed
Reading–Thinking Activity

◆ ◆ ◆

The Directed Reading–Thinking Activity (DR-TA) is a reading strategy used to introduce a reading selection and to encourage students to form predictions as a means of making their reading more purposeful. It was proposed by Stauffer (1980) as an alternative to the DRA, one that places the responsibility for setting purposes on the students. Doing so, he claimed, would make them more purposeful readers. The steps of a DR-TA are simple to plan. The first and last steps are identical to those of the DRA.

Step 1. Develop readiness for the reading selection. Try to anticipate deficiencies in prior knowledge of the content and then shore them up by introducing vocabulary, providing factual information, offering visual aids, etc.

Step 2. Ask the students to read to a key point and then stop. They are then to form predictions about how the story will end. These predictions may be generated individually or by collaborative groups.

Step 3. Permit the students to read the remainder of the story for the purpose of testing their predictions.

Step 4. Lead a discussion, focusing on the predictions students have made. Were they right or wrong? Why?

Step 5. Provide extension or reinforcement activities. These can take many forms and could focus on word recognition, comprehension, or personal responses to content.

The DR-TA lacks some of the flexibility of the DRA. It can be used only with materials that lend themselves to making predictions, and this usually means fiction or narrative nonfiction. It would not be suitable for most textbook selections. On the other hand, the DR-TA is less teacher centered than the DRA, and research evidence of its effectiveness is convincing.

READ MORE ABOUT IT

◆ ◆ ◆

Stauffer, Russell. (1980). *The language experience approach to the teaching of reading* (2nd ed.). New York: Harper & Row.

Tierney, Robert J., and Readence, John E. (2000). *Reading strategies and practices: A compendium* (5th ed.). Boston: Allyn & Bacon.

K-W-L

♦ ♦ ♦

K-W-L is a strategy used to encourage students to set their own purposes for reading nonfiction. It also allows a teacher to activate background knowledge and assess its adequacy at the same time. The three steps of K-W-L are simple to apply, though they can be time consuming. In the first step, students share what they already <u>K</u>now about a subject. In the second step, they suggest what they <u>W</u>ant to learn. In the third step, they review what they have actually <u>L</u>earned.

Step 1. Briefly tell the students about the topic they will be studying. Ask them to tell you what they already know about it. This will lead to a brainstorming session in which words, phrases and short sentences will be offered by students. Record them in the "K" column of a K-W-L chart, which you can create on the board or project as a transparency. (See the blank chart masters on the pages at the end of this chapter.)

Step 2. Ask the students what they would like to learn from the reading selection (usually a textbook chapter or nonfiction trade book). Record these in the "W" column of the chart. These questions become the purpose for reading. You may need to provide subtle prompts in order to nudge students into mentioning important ideas that you know are contained in the material.

Step 3. After the reading, return to the "W" column and discuss which of the questions have actually been answered in the selection. Those that remain unanswered will need to be researched or simply answered by the teacher.

K-W-L has the advantage of being student centered and naturally engaging. It also underscores the link between new learning and old. On the other hand, it is limited to nonfiction and does not work well with highly unfamiliar material since the students may know little or nothing at the outset.

READ MORE ABOUT IT

◆ ◆ ◆

Ogle, Donna. (1986). K-W-L: A teaching model that develops active reading of expository text. *The Reading Teacher, 39,* 564–570.

Tierney, Robert J., and Readence, John E. (2000). *Reading strategies and practices: A compendium* (5th ed.). Boston: Allyn & Bacon. [Call 800-666-9433]

K-W-L

What do you Know?	What do you Want to know?	What have you Learned?

From *Help for Struggling Readers* by Michael C. McKenna. Copyright 2002 by The Guilford Press. Permission to photocopy this page is granted to purchasers of this book for personal use only (see copyright page for details).

K-W-L

What do you Know?	What do you Want to know?	What have you Learned?

From *Help for Struggling Readers* by Michael C. McKenna. Copyright 2002 by The Guilford Press. Permission to photocopy this page is granted to purchasers of this book for personal use only (see copyright page for details).

Listen–Read–Discuss

◆ ◆ ◆

Listen–Read–Discuss is a reading lesson format especially designed for struggling readers. Its three stages represent the before, during, and after stages of all reading lesson formats. Listen–Read–Discuss is markedly different from the Directed Reading Activity or the Directed Reading–Thinking Activity, however, because of its first step. During the Listen phase of the lesson, the teacher completely presents the content, almost as though there was to be no reading at all on the part of the students. Doing so boosts prior knowledge to a very high level, making the reading itself much easier. The following steps constitute the entire approach:

Step 1. Present the content of the reading selection thoroughly. Use lecture, discussion, demonstration, and whatever other techniques promise to be effective.

Step 2. Have students read the selection. Provide them with specific purposes, just as you would in a DRA.

Step 3. Lead a discussion based on the purpose-setting activity you provided.

Listen–Read–Discuss may not sound like the most exciting instructional approach ever devised. It isn't. But its background-building capacity more than makes up for this deficit. Students report learning much more through Listen–Read–Discuss than through alternative approaches, and test results support their claims. Reading is almost like a review since new concepts and ideas have already been thoroughly introduced. Decoding is also facilitated since new terms are pronounced and written on the board during the Listen stage.

READ MORE ABOUT IT

◆ ◆ ◆

Manzo, Anthony V., and Casale, Ula P. (1985). Listen–Read–Discuss: A content reading heuristic. *Journal of Reading, 28,* 732–734.

McKenna, Michael C., and Robinson, Richard D. (2002). *Teaching through text: A content literacy approach to content area reading* (3rd ed.). New York: Longman.

SECTION 5

◆ ◆ ◆

Questioning Strategies

Levels of Questions

◆ ◆ ◆

Asking questions not only stimulates comprehension during class discussions but also helps teachers monitor how (and if!) students have constructed meaning from what they have read. Thinking about *levels* of questions and asking them strategically, with the level in mind, offers great flexibility. By posing questions at various levels of thinking, a teacher can get a glimpse of how the child has processed a reading selection and encourage higher-order thinking at the same time.

There are many ways of categorizing questions by level. Bloom's Taxonomy is sometimes used, for example. But a far simpler approach is to think of questions in terms of three fundamental levels of comprehension.

1. *Literal questions* require a student to recall a specific fact that has been explicitly stated in the reading selection. Such questions are easy to ask and answer, but they may reflect a very superficial understanding of content. Edgar Dale, an eminent reading authority during the first half of the 20th century, once referred to literal comprehension as "reading the lines."

2. *Inferential questions*, like literal questions, have factual answers. However, the answers cannot be located in the selection. Instead of finding the answer, the reader must make logical connections among facts in order to arrive at an answer. The question calling for a prediction, for example, is always inferential in nature even though we are uncertain of the answer, for the reader must nevertheless use available facts in an effort to arrive at a fact that is not stated. The answers to inferential questions are sometimes beyond dispute and at other times quite speculative. Let's say that a class has just read a selection on New Zealand. They have read that New Zealand is south of the equator and was colonized by Great Britain. If a teacher were to ask whether Auckland, New Zealand's capital, is south of the equator, the question would be inferential. There is no dispute about the answer, but the selection does not specifically address the relationship of Auckland to the equator. The students must infer it. On the other hand, were the teacher to ask the students if they think that English is spoken in New Zealand, this

question too is inferential. However, the answer is more speculative. The mere fact that Britain colonized New Zealand does not guarantee that English is spoken there today. For all inferential questions, the reader must use facts that are stated to reach a conclusion about a fact that is not stated. For this reason, Dale described inferential comprehension as "reading between the lines."

3. *Critical questions* call upon students to form value judgments about the selection. Such judgments can never be characterized as right or wrong, accurate or inaccurate. This is because the answers to critical questions are not facts. They are judgments arrived at on the basis of an individual's value system. Critical questions might target whether the selection is well written, whether certain topics should have been included, whether the arguments an author makes are valid, and whether the writing is biased or objective. Understandably, Edgar Dale equated critical comprehension with "reading beyond the lines." (*Hint*: A shortcut to asking a critical-level question is to insert the word *should*. This always elevates the question to the critical level. Of course, there are other ways to pose critical questions, but this method is surefire!)

Read the following excerpt on the planet Pluto, taken from an eighth-grade science text. Consider each of the following questions in light of the information presented in the text. Can you classify each of these questions?

1. What is the temperature on Pluto?
2. Is there life on Pluto?
3. Should the United States fund a space mission to Pluto?

The first question is literal because the temperature is clearly stated. As one of my middle grade students once put it, "It's a Christopher Columbus question because you can find the answer and land on it!"

The second question is inferential because, even though the existence of life is not mentioned, the question does have a factual answer. Moreover, the authors give several facts that help us make a defensible inference (it's cold on Pluto, there's no atmosphere and little light). Students sometimes think such questions are unfair because they call for conjecture and the answers cannot simply be "landed on." You may need to broaden their perspectives a bit! And remember, the vast majority of questions on standardized achievement tests are inferential in nature!

The third question is critical. (Note the word *should*!) Reasonable people may disagree about the answer, which is not a fact but a critical judgment.

Pluto

– Pluto has been described as a "snowball," a mix of frozen methane and ammonia with a surface temperature of −237° C (−395° F). It has no atmosphere. The smallest planet, about the size of Earth's moon, Pluto has an irregular orbit that sometimes takes it inside Neptune's orbit. For example, between 1979 and 1999, Neptune will be the outermost planet in the solar system, not Pluto.

Pluto rotates so slowly on its axis that one day equals six Earth-days plus nine hours and eighteen minutes. During the day on Pluto, the sun appears like a bright star. Indeed, many stars are apparent in Pluto's dusk-like daytime sky. This planet takes nearly 250 Earth-years to make one revolution around the sun. Its one moon is about half its own size. Pluto has a slight gravitational pull, about one-tenth of Earth's.

Math ⚡ Link
You're How Old?

How many Earth-days old would you be if you were born 13 Venus-years ago? How many Earth-years would that amount to? How many Earth-years older would you be after living on Neptune for two of its years? If you met an 18-year-old person from Venus and a 20-year-old person from Pluto, how old would they be in Earth-years?

Illustration not to scale

Sun

Pluto

An illustration of what Pluto might look like from its moon Charon

Charon

Source: Atwater, Mary, Baptiste, Prentice, Daniel, Lucy, Hackett, Jay, Moyer, Richard, Takemoto, Carol, and Wilson, Nancy. (1995). *Science.* New York: Macmillan/McGraw-Hill. Copyright 1995 by Macmillan/McGraw-Hill Scool Publishing Company. Reprinted by permission.

Question–Answer Relationships

◆ ◆ ◆

In Question–Answer Relationships (QARs), Raphael suggests that students should be "let in" on the fact that different types of questions exist and that each type requires a different reading strategy. The four types of QARs are named with student-friendly designations as follows:

In-the-Book-QARs

Right There   These are literal-level questions, and the answers can be found in the material. Indeed, they are "right there."

Think and Search   These are inferential questions that require students to make logical connections among the facts presented in the material.

In-My-Head-QARs

Author and You   The reader must combine information from the material with prior knowledge.

On My Own   These are questions that rely almost entirely on students' prior knowledge and experience. This category includes critical-level questions.

These types roughly correspond to the literal, inferential, and critical levels of comprehension. Let's look at a simple example of the four types. The following brief passage easily leads to such questions.

The three basic rock types include igneous, metamorphic, and sedimentary. Igneous rocks, such as basalt and obsidian, were once molten. Metamorphic rocks, like marble and granite, were formed by a combination of heat and pressure. Sedimentary rocks, such as limestone and shale, were the result of slow deposits beneath bodies of water.

Right There	"What is one type of sedimentary rock?"
Think and Search	"Were sedimentary rocks ever molten?
Author and You	"What type of rock might you find near a volcano?"
On My Own	"Which type of rock do you think is most plentiful?"

QARs can help students recognize that comprehension is not limited to the literal level, at which answers are routinely regurgitated. Disputing question types can be healthy, but don't press the point too far.

TIPS FOR USING QARS

Students must be introduced to QARs systematically. Some teachers recommend a three-stage process.

1. *Teacher defines and models*. Select short passages from reading selections and create clear-cut examples of each question type. Define the four types of QARs in simple terms and introduce examples to help clarify differences. In later selections interject examples at certain points, again pointing out how they conform to the definition of one of the four types.

2. *Students classify*. In subsequent reading selections, pose questions of each type and ask students to classify them. They will need to locate the answer, or the basis of the answer, before they can do so, of course. Provide numerous opportunities for students to classify questions of each type. Give feedback and encourage discussion, even if classifying some questions seems a bit murky.

3. *Students generate*. Once students fully grasp the distinctions among the four types of questions, ask them to create their own examples, either individually or collaboratively. Use the chart at the end of this chapter, created by Claire Smith while a middle school teacher in Winder, Georgia. Share the questions in class and require students to defend their classifications.

READ MORE ABOUT IT
◆ ◆ ◆

Raphael, Taffy E. (1984). Teaching learners about sources of information for answering comprehension questions. *Journal of Reading, 27,* 303–311.

Tierney, Robert J., and Readence, John E. (2000). *Reading strategies and practices: A compendium* (5th ed.). Boston: Allyn & Bacon.

Question-Answer Relationships

RIGHT THERE	AUTHOR & YOU
Answer is in the text	*Answer is NOT in the text*

THINK & SEARCH	ON MY OWN
Put together different parts of the story.	*Use my own experience*

From *Help for Struggling Readers* by Michael C. McKenna. Copyright 2002 by The Guilford Press. Permission to photocopy this page is granted to purchasers of this book for personal use only (see copyright page for details). This chart was created by Claire Smith and is reprinted here with her permission.

Question Clusters

◆ ◆ ◆

Effective teachers often ask several questions with a single end in mind. By clustering questions in this way, you can lead a more focused discussion and help to foster a better understanding of the content of a reading selection. Five types of question clusters are described here. Each has a special use, and each is easy to apply whenever the situation is appropriate.

The example provided here for each type of question cluster is based on the story "The Worst Bank Robbers," published in *The Book of Failures* by Stephen Pile. Read the story first, then read about the types of clusters and how the examples represent each type.

The Worst Bank Robbers

In August 1975 three men were on their way to rob the Royal Bank of Scotland at Rothesay, when they got stuck in the revolving doors. They had to be helped free by the staff and, after thanking everyone, sheepishly left the building.

A few minutes later they returned and announced their intention of robbing the bank, but none of the staff believed them. When, at first, they demanded £5,000, the head cashier laughed at them, convinced that it was a practical joke.

Considerably disheartened by this, the gang leader reduced his demand first to £500, then to £50 and ultimately to 50 pence. By this stage the cashier could barely control herself for laughter.

Then one of the men jumped over the counter and fell awkwardly on the floor, clutching at his ankle. The other two made their getaway, but got trapped in the revolving doors for a second time, desperately pushing the wrong way.

BOTTOM-UP CLUSTER

One or more literal-level questions are followed by a higher-level question. The higher-level question can call for either an inference or a critical judgment. Answers to the lit-

103

eral questions help the students answer the higher-level question. This cluster targets struggling readers specifically and shows them how to think more critically about what they read.

TEACHER: What happened when the men entered the bank the first time?

STUDENT: They got caught in the door.

TEACHER: Yes, and what happened when they asked for the money?

STUDENT: They were laughed at.

TEACHER: Right. And when they left?

STUDENT: They got caught in the door again.

TEACHER: Do you think they were good at robbing banks?

TOP-DOWN CLUSTER

A higher-level question is followed by one or more literal-level questions. This is a "trouble-shooting" cluster, used when a student is unable to answer a higher-level question, or answers inappropriately. Once the literal-level questions have been answered, the teacher returns to the original, higher-level question. The bottom-up cluster above might have been reversed to form a top-down cluster:

TEACHER: Do you think these men were good at robbing banks?

STUDENT: Well, I guess so. They were professionals.

TEACHER: What happened when the men entered the bank the first time?

STUDENT: They got caught in the door.

TEACHER: Yes, and what happened when they asked for the money?

STUDENT: They were laughed at.

TEACHER: Right. And when they left?

STUDENT: They got caught in the door again.

TEACHER: Do you still say they were good at robbing banks?

CLARIFYING CLUSTER

When an answer is vague or uses language that may not be clear to other students, follow-up questions are asked to make sure all of the students understand the answer to the initial question.

TEACHER: Why did the cashier laugh at the men?

STUDENT: She thought it was a prank.

TEACHER: What's a prank?

STUDENT: You know, a trick, a joke.

EXTENDING CLUSTER

Here, a student has responded appropriately, but the teacher wishes to elicit additional thinking. The same student or other students might be asked for alternative answers.

TEACHER: After they had trouble with the door, why might it have been smarter for the robbers to give up on their plan?

STUDENT 1: They might have expected the reaction they got.

TEACHER: Yes. Any other reasons?

STUDENT 2: They might have expected more trouble with the door.

TEACHER: Right! Anyone else?

STUDENT 3: The employees had had too good a look at them.

SLICING CLUSTER

In slicing, the scope of a question may be too broad for the student. It is reworded to ask for less information. In other words, it is cut down to size.

TEACHER: Who can tell me each of the amounts the robbers demanded? (*No answer.*)

TEACHER: OK, what was the first amount they asked for?

STUDENT: £5,000.

These examples illustrate how clustering questions in order to reach a particular goal can enhance a discussion by helping students arrive at desirable conclusions without spoon-feeding them. All of the clusters except the bottom-up are created on the spot, as they are needed. The bottom-up cluster must be planned in advance.

READ MORE ABOUT IT

♦ ♦ ♦

McKenna, Michael C., and Robinson, Richard D. (2002). *Teaching through text: A content literacy approach to content area reading* (3rd ed.). New York: Longman.

Reciprocal Questioning

◆ ◆ ◆

Manzo's technique of Reciprocal Questioning (ReQuest) has now been effectively used for more than three decades. It involves students actively asking questions of the teacher during a discussion. The basic idea is that in order to ask good questions a reader must understand the content reasonably well. If a reader reads with the aim of asking questions, then comprehension is apt to be good. In the years following its introduction, research has continually validated ReQuest, and many variations of the technique have sprung up.

VARIATION 1

The teacher introduces the reading selection and asks the students to begin reading silently. At a predesignated point the students stop reading, and one student is called on to ask questions of the teacher. The teacher must answer as many questions as the student can think to ask. When the student can think of no more questions, the teacher asks the student additional questions. For the next segment of the reading selection, another student is called on.

VARIATION 2

After the selection has been completed, the teacher calls on a student at random. The student asks the teacher one question and the teacher asks the student a question. The teacher then calls on another student, and so forth.

VARIATION 3

The teacher begins the postreading discussion by calling on a student. The student asks a question but, instead of answering it, the teacher deflects it to another student, who must try to answer. This second student may then ask a question, which the teacher reflects to a third student, and so forth. The teacher may use his or her knowledge of students' abilities to decide which questions to deflect to which students.

READ MORE ABOUT IT

♦ ♦ ♦

McKenna, Michael C., and Robinson, Richard D. (2002). *Teaching through text: A content literacy approach to content area reading* (3rd ed.). New York: Longman.

Tierney, Robert J., and Readence, John E. (2000). *Reading strategies and practices: A compendium* (5th ed.). Boston: Allyn & Bacon.

Questioning the Author

♦ ♦ ♦

Prompting students to grasp the meaning of nonfiction is a formidable challenge to teachers in the upper elementary and middle grades. This is hardly the same as memorizing and later "regurgitating" superficial facts. Questioning the Author (QtA) is a strategy designed to help students truly make sense of the new content they encounter in nonfiction, although Isabel Beck and her colleagues point out that QtA is useful with fiction as well.

The central idea behind QtA is that questions should be posed during reading, not afterward. In this way, a teacher can ensure that students actively consider important issues as they encounter appropriate passages. Beck et al. (1997) summarize QtA this way:

> As text is read in class, the teacher intervenes at selected points and poses queries to prompt students to consider information in the text. Students respond by contributing ideas, which may be built upon, refined, or challenged by other students and by the teacher. Finally, students and the teacher work collaboratively, interacting to grapple with ideas and build understanding. (p. 8)

A typical QtA lesson involves

- ♦ Deciding in advance where the text should be segmented.
- ♦ Stopping after each segment to pose "queries" designed to prompt thinking (as opposed to traditional "questions," aimed primarily at assessment).
- ♦ Encouraging students to discuss confusing points in a risk-free atmosphere.
- ♦ Striving for answers that go beyond reciting explicit factual statements.

108

- Challenging the author, where appropriate, as the ultimate authority on the content.
- Moving back and forth between the text and class discussion.
- Proceeding from one segment to the next.

EXAMPLE

Let's use the brief passage that follows as an example of several important aspects of QtA.

The Vikings explored the North Atlantic region, moving westward from island to island. From their homes in Scandinavia, they reached Ireland, England, Iceland and Greenland. Then, five hundred years before the voyages of Columbus, the Vikings visited North America. In the year 987, a fleet of Viking ships came within sight of what is now Canada, and in the year 1000 Lief Erikson and his crew landed in the New World. The Vikings settled briefly in North America, but after a short time they left, never realizing that they had reached the edge of a vast continent.

Let's consider three questions the teacher might ask once the students have read this paragraph.

1. In what year did Lief Erikson land in North America?
2. What does the author mean by saying the Vikings moved "westward from island to island"?
3. What is the author really telling us about the Vikings?
4. Why do you think the Vikings left the New World?
5. Why do you think five centuries passed between the Vikings and Columbus without anyone crossing the Atlantic from Europe?
6. Has the author left out important facts you'd like to know about the Vikings?

In this example, Question 1 represents a traditional, literal-level question designed to assess whether the students have "picked up" this factual detail. The point of QtA is that students can often answer such questions without truly understanding the significance of what they are reading. Beck and her colleagues underscore the difference between this and the questions they recommend by using the word query. Queries 2 and 3 are *initiating queries*, aimed at starting the discussion on a meaningful level by prompting students to think beyond the facts presented in the paragraph. Queries 4, 5 and 6 are *follow-up queries*, encouraging students to make connections between facts they encounter in the text and their own prior knowledge. Notice how Query 6 challenges the author's position as the ultimate decision maker concerning what information to present.

PLANNING A QtA LESSON

Beck et al. (1997) recommend several steps in preparing a QtA lesson.

Step 1. Read the text selection closely, determining the major ideas students need to construct and identifying probable trouble spots. In our example about the Vikings, the teacher might well conclude that students might have little familiarity with Iceland and Greenland and might also have difficulty envisioning the westward movement of the Vikings without a map.

Step 2. Decide where to segment the selection. Beck and her colleagues emphasize that this decision is not driven by paragraph breaks but by the understandings the teacher decides the students must derive. This guiding principle may mean discussing a single paragraph or grouping several paragraphs together before pausing to discuss.

Step 3. Develop queries. For each segment, the teacher must decide in advance what initiating queries to pose and how students are likely to respond. The teacher must also develop follow-up queries in an effort to help students link ideas. Of course, the later segments present more opportunities for such links.

In planning, the teacher looks for overarching themes and ideas. Facts are seen as instrumental in helping students mentally construct these themes.

CHARACTERISTICS OF A QtA DISCUSSION

Discussion in a QtA lesson differs considerably from a conventional class discussion. As Beck et al. (1997) explain, "the teacher's role involves participating in thinking and helping students develop ideas rather than managing thinking and explaining ideas" (p. 77). It is important for the teacher to empathize with the limitations and problems students face as they encounter text content, something stressed in planning a QtA lesson (see Step 1). Unlike a conventional discussion, in which the teacher does most of the work in constructing meaning, the teacher uses queries to guide students in constructing their own meanings.

Several practices help keep the discussion productive without wresting control of the meaning-making process away from students. These practices are called marking, turning back, revoicing, modeling, annotating, and recapping.

When a student raises an important point, the teacher may wish to *mark* it by restating it or by explicitly calling attention to its significance. If Ben were to comment that the Vikings didn't seem content with where they originally lived, the teacher might say, "Yes, it seems the Vikings needed to explore."

When a student provides an answer that is limited or vague, the teacher may decide to *turn back* responsibility for the issue to the student. This is done by asking for an elaboration of the first answer. Turning back also means getting students to make connections. For example, Beth might mention how briefly the Vikings stayed in North America. In QtA, the teacher might turn back this issue by asking, "How does this relate to what Ben said?"

Occasionally, the teacher will find it useful to *revoice* what students have been struggling to express. "So the Vikings kept on moving, like jumping around, maybe looking for the best place," Julio says. "Right," Lakesha adds, "they kept sailing to the west." The teacher might revoice these thoughts by saying, "So you could say that they sailed west, from one island to the next, just seeing what they could find."

Sometimes it is important for the teacher to *model* productive thinking about a passage. Modeling of this kind is similar to a think-aloud in that it provides students with a glimpse of how good readers actively process text content. Such modeling might focus on some affective response to the text: "You know these Vikings must have been very brave. They sailed into unknown parts of the world in small wooden boats. You'd never have caught me doing that!" Modeling might target possible points of confusion: "Hmm, when the author says the Vikings 'came within sight of what is now Canada,' that must mean that Canada didn't exist back then." Modeling might also aim at larger issues: "You know what I'm wondering? I'm wondering why the people in Europe didn't start coming across to America after the Vikings arrived here. After all, that's what happened after Columbus arrived. Right?"

From time to time, the teacher will find it useful to *annotate* the discussion. This means providing factual information that can fill in gaps in the content presented in the text. "Here's a picture I found of a Viking ship," the teacher might say, or "The author tells us the Vikings lived in Scandinavia. Now, Scandinavia isn't really a country. It's a large area of northern Europe. Let's find it on our wall map."

Finally, discussion of a text segment might conclude with a *recap*. "Nice work," the teacher might conclude, "You've managed to tell how the Vikings explored their world and why." Beck and her colleagues point out that the students themselves might be called upon to recap the ideas expressed in a segment. "Who can tell us in a few words where the Vikings started and where they went from there?"

CONDUCTING A QtA LESSON

Because QtA differs markedly from conventional approaches to reading and discussing, some suggestions may make the transition easier.

- ◆ Arrange the desks in a U shape to facilitate discussion.
- ◆ If students are not yet used to QtA, explain that they will be taking part in something new. Suggest that sometimes reading difficulties are the fault of the author. As a class, you will be trying to discover what the author was trying to say but may not have succeeded very well in saying.
- ◆ Try presenting a brief passage to show students how QtA will work.

A FINAL WORD

QtA represents a different manner of conceptualizing how students should interact with text. It provides them with continuous support, especially with trouble spots. Best of all, it compels students to process text deeply, interpreting an author's intent and occasionally challenging the authority of the text. Empirical studies of QtA have verified its effectiveness as a tool for improving comprehension in fourth grade and higher. QtA, or adaptations of it, can almost certainly be used with success as early as second grade.

READ MORE ABOUT IT

◆ ◆ ◆

Beck, Isabel L., McKeown, Margaret G., Hamilton, Rebecca L., and Kucan, Linda. (1997). *Questioning the author: An approach for enhancing student engagement with text*. Newark, DE: International Reading Association.

SECTION 6

◆ ◆ ◆

Other Comprehension Strategies

Specific Skill Approaches

◆ ◆ ◆

A time-honored approach to improving comprehension ability is to subdivide the broad and rather murky area of comprehension into specific skills. There are advantages to doing so, to be sure. It makes comprehension instruction more manageable and facilitates planning. It is also conducive to clear-cut activities that focus on a particular skill or set of skills.

On the other hand, teaching comprehension one skill at a time poses a few problems. It can delude a teacher into thinking that comprehension is the sum of these subskills and that teaching them will inevitably produce a good comprehender. Comprehension is more than the sum of its parts, however. The subskill approach also presents measurement problems. Scores on tests designed to measure one skill are highly correlated with those geared toward another skill. Because comprehension skills are tied to general comprehension ability, it is impossible to separate them for assessment. Finally, organizing instruction around subskills invites a reliance on worksheets and tedious drill. It is vital to resist this temptation.

When prudently planned, specific skill approaches can yield very positive results. Here is one breakdown of comprehension, first into the three levels and then into specific skills.*

Literal level	Inferential level	Critical level
Explicit sequence	Implicit sequence	Judgment of adequacy
Explicit cause and effect	Implicit cause and effect	Judgment of validity
Explicit comparison	Implicit comparison	Judgment of fantasy versus reality
Explicit character trait	Implicit character trait	Detection of propaganda
Explicit main idea	Implicit main idea	Judgment of literary quality
	Predicting an outcome	
	Interpreting figurative language	
	Identifying a pronoun antecedent	
	Discerning an anaphoric relationship	

*Source: Miller, John W., and McKenna, Michael C. (1989). *Teaching reading in the elementary classroom.* Scottsdale, AZ: Gorsuch Scarisbrick.

115

Walk-Throughs

◆ ◆ ◆

An excellent prereading activity for nonfiction selections is the walk-through. The teacher briefly discusses the organization of the selection page by page as the students follow along in their own copies. The teacher "walks them through" the material, in other words, giving them an idea of what to expect. To use another analogy, the walk-through provides the skeleton of the selection, while the reading itself puts flesh on the bones.

The walk-through is based on Robert Aukerman's Survey Technique (1972). His goal was to adapt the first step of the SQ3R study technique for use with a class. He recommended that the teacher lead the students in doing the following:

1. Analyze the chapter title and try to predict what might be included.
2. Analyze subheadings.
3. Analyze visual aids (graphs, charts, maps, pictures, etc.)
4. Read and discuss the first paragraph.
5. Read and discuss the last paragraph.
6. Read and discuss (briefly) postreading questions.
7. Try to infer the main idea of the chapter.

Here are some suggestions for making walk-throughs more effective when introducing nonfiction selections in your own classroom:

◆ Hold up your copy of the text as you discuss it. Students will be able to look back and forth from your copy to theirs so that they can tell exactly what you are describing.
◆ Ask questions that engage the students from time to time during your discussion. A walk-through should not be all teacher talk. You must be sure that students are following along as you speak. Questions that call for predictions can be especially

effective, such as "From this subtitle, what do you think this section will be about?"

♦ Be sure to point out interesting features of the material. Unusual facts or graphics can kindle interest.

♦ Don't ignore sidebars and graphics aids. These are integral to the material, even though there may be a tendency to ignore them if you concentrate too much on the linear presentation of content. Also, sidebars, while visually appealing, can be confusing to young readers. Help them navigate successfully.

♦ Try combining walk-throughs with reading guides. You can introduce the guide and the organization of the material at the same time. Such a practice combines two of the most effective content literacy instructional techniques.

Walk-throughs are easily combined with other techniques. As a prereading strategy, they can be included in a directed reading activity, K-W-L, Listen–Read–Discuss, and other lesson formats. They are a central part of Guided Reading in Textual Settings (GRITS), described on pp. 149–152.

Walk-throughs enjoy considerable empirical support. Donna Alvermann and her colleagues (Alvermann & Moore, 1991; Alvermann & Swafford, 1989) examined walk-throughs and gave the technique very high marks.

READ MORE ABOUT IT

♦ ♦ ♦

Alvermann, Donna E., & Moore, David W. (1991). Secondary school reading. In R. Barr, M. L. Kamil, P. B. Mosenthal, & P. D. Pearson (Eds.), *Handbook of reading research* (Vol. 2, pp. 951–983). White Plains, NY: Longman.

Alvermann, Donna E., & Swafford, Jeanne. (1989). Do content area strategies have a research base? *Journal of Reading, 32,* 388–394.

Aukerman, Robert C. (1972). *Reading in the secondary school.* New York: McGraw-Hill.

Readence, John E., Moore, David W., and Rickelman, Robert J. (2000). *Prereading activities for content area reading and learning* (3rd ed.). Newark, DE: International Reading Association.

Think-Alouds

◆ ◆ ◆

A think-aloud is a technique through which a teacher models how to handle a comprehension problem that arises during reading. For example, Ms. Williams, a social studies teacher, reads aloud a brief passage from the textbook. The passage contains these sentences:

> George Washington fought on the side of the British during the French and Indian War. Years later he would fight against the British during the American Revolution.

As soon as Ms. Williams reads the words "George Washington fought on the side of the British," she pauses and says, "Wait a minute. I thought George Washington fought *against* the British. That doesn't make sense, does it? Maybe if we keep reading the author will explain." And, of course, reading on does clear up the problem.

Proficient readers (such as yourself) continually find themselves in minor comprehension predicaments of this kind. What distinguishes them from struggling readers, however, is the fact that good readers can apply strategies for "fixing" such problems. These "fix-up" strategies include:

1. Reading ahead to see if the problem can be resolved.
2. Rereading to see if something has been misunderstood.
3. Reflecting on what has been read to see if some alternative explanation can be inferred.
4. Seeking information beyond the text (from an individual or a second print source) in order to resolve the dilemma.

In a think-aloud, a teacher models this "fix-up" process by exposing it aloud. In the words of Scott Paris, the teacher "makes thinking public" so that students are privy to how a proficient reader contends with problem situations.

Think-alouds began as a research tool through which the thought processes of struggling readers were studied. The instructional value of think-alouds soon became apparent, however, and they now constitute a thoroughly validated way of helping students monitor and improve their comprehension.

An advantage of think-alouds is that they are nested within other instruction. They are quick to use and in no way divert attention away from the reading selection. Plus, think-alouds tend to enliven a teacher's oral reading, making it more engaging and accessible to students.

Here are some tips for using think-alouds while reading to students.

♦ Plan your think-alouds ahead of time. They may seem spontaneous to students, and you may be able to make them work on a spur-of-the-moment basis, but a little planning can smooth the rough edges.

♦ Look for canned think-alouds in your teacher's edition. Think-alouds are so popular and effective that textbook authors frequently provide suggested think-alouds at key points.

♦ Occasionally stop a student who is reading aloud at a critical point. Ask the student whether the material makes sense and what he or she might do about it. In other words, encourage the student to think aloud.

READ MORE ABOUT IT

♦ ♦ ♦

Oster, L. (2001). Using the think-aloud for reading instruction. *The Reading Teacher, 55*, 64–75.

Tierney, Robert J., and Readence, John E. (2000). *Reading strategies and practices: A compendium* (5th ed.). Boston: Allyn & Bacon.

Imaging

◆ ◆ ◆

Some teachers find it difficult to see how some students find it difficult to see—with their mind's eye, that is! Forming a mental picture of what we read is vital to comprehension, especially of narrative text. In a large study conducted at Vanderbilt University, researchers discovered that the inability to form mental images was one of two major problems experienced by struggling middle schoolers. (The other was poor decoding.)

Instruction *can* assist children in forming images. Here are brief overviews of three research-based approaches.

APPROACH 1: INDUCED IMAGERY

Linda Gambrell's Induced Imagery technique uses teacher modeling to encourage children to form mental pictures as they read. She has suggested a three-step process:

1. *Teacher modeling.* Select a short descriptive paragraph and distribute it or create a transparency. Make your purpose clear by explaining how forming mental pictures helps us understand and remember what we read. Read the paragraph aloud while students follow along. Then share your own image, saying, "Now here's what I see in my mind. . . . "

2. *Guided practice.* Provide additional short descriptive paragraphs. Ask students to form their own mental pictures as they read. Encourage students to discuss and compare their images. Stress that there is no single correct image but that some details should overlap.

3. *Independent practice.* Occasionally choose passages from other materials children are reading and remind them to form images. Conduct brief discussions on these occasions. Encourage them to apply imaging in other situations as well, such as content area reading and leisure reading.

APPROACH 2: VISUALIZE–VERBALIZE

The Lindamoods have taken an alternate route to improved imaging. Their procedure involves accumulating a large number of pictures to be kept in a folder or portfolio. (For more information about visualize–verbalize, visit www.lindamoodbell.com.) They can come from any source, such as magazines, newspapers, the Internet, etc. The procedure (slightly modified) then works like this:

1. Begin by modeling the process. Select a picture, but do not show it to the class. Tell the students you want to create in their minds the very picture you alone can see. As you look at it, describe it in as much detail as possible.
2. When you finish, reveal the picture. Discuss how students' images may have differed from the actual picture and how they were similar.
3. Next, have a student select a picture at random, with no one seeing it.
4. Ask the student to look at the picture but not to show it to the teacher or the rest of the class.
5. The student's task is to describe the picture in as much detail as possible so that the others can form a mental image.
6. You, of course, are already familiar with the picture. When the student runs out of comments, ask prompting questions about overlooked details.
7. Finally, the picture is revealed, and a brief discussion focuses on details that may have been neglected and about how the other students' mental images differ from the real one.

While the main thrust of the approach is on reading, it offers a hidden benefit in the area of writing. The student who describes the picture engages in a form of composition, even though print is not involved. The same attention to detail is required in converting a real object into language. Over time, students' descriptions become more elaborate, and less prompting is needed.

APPROACH 3: MONSTER EXCHANGE

This age-appropriate technique stimulates creativity by building on an existing interest—monsters! Better yet, students find themselves writing thorough descriptive paragraphs without even knowing that's what they're doing. Here's all you do:

1. Instruct each student to draw a monster, being as creative as possible.
2. Ask each student to write a description of the monster. The description must be detailed enough that someone else can use it to draw the same monster without having seen the picture.
3. Remind each student to put his/her name on both the picture and the paragraph.
4. Arrange for the students to swap paragraphs.

5. Provide time for each student to draw a second monster, based on the written description.

6. Pair the students and allow them to compare the original pictures with those drawn on the basis of the descriptions.

7. Encourage discussion, focusing on details that were left out by the writer or ignored by the reader.

READ MORE ABOUT IT
◆ ◆ ◆

Gambrell, Linda, and Bales, R. J. (1984). Mental imagery and the comprehension monitoring performance of fourth- and fifth-grade poor readers. *Reading Research Quarterly, 21,* 454–464.

Gambrell, Linda, and Jawitz, P. B. (1993). Mental imagery text illustrations and children's story comprehension and recall. *Reading Research Quarterly, 28,* 264–273.

Gambrell, Linda, Kapinus, Barbara A., and Wilson, R. M. (1987). Using mental imagery and summarization to achieve independence in comprehension. *Journal of Reading, 30,* 638–642.

Teaching with Analogies

◆ ◆ ◆

Analogies are comparisons of two unrelated ideas that are similar in some ways. One of the ideas is familiar, the other unfamiliar. Analogies can be extremely useful in explaining abstract new content to students because they provide a means of linking new ideas to prior knowledge. The result is that understanding is enhanced and retention improved.

Shawn Glynn has suggested a method teachers can use to bring new content to life through analogies. His six-step method (TWA) is easy to use and gives structure to the lesson:

Step 1. Introduce the concept to be learned.
Step 2. Review the analogous concept.
Step 3. Identify features that both concepts possess.
Step 4. Explain the similarities.
Step 5. Discuss where the analogy breaks down.
Step 6. Draw conclusions.

Glynn's research confirmed that students' comprehension of new ideas was substantially improved by this process when all six steps were followed (Glynn, 1989, 1995, 1996). Let's examine these steps in the context of an example.

EXAMPLE: PHOTOSYNTHESIS

1. *Introduce the concept to be learned.* The teacher defines the term *photosynthesis* and provides background information. Graphic organizers might be used, such as time lines and labeled pictures.

2. *Review the analogous concept.* The analogy involves a factory. The teacher engages the students in a discussion of how a factory operates, possibly using a local example. (For our example, let's consider a paper factory.) The teacher stresses how energy and raw materials are converted in the factory into some sort of desirable good.

3. *Identify features that both concepts possess.* The teacher lists elements common to both photosynthesis and a factory. They both use energy, start with raw materials, produce a desirable finished product, and create waste products along the way.

4. *Explain the similarities.* The teacher lists these elements in chart form. At this point the specifics of each concept are included. Such a chart might look like this:

	Photosynthesis	Paper factory
Raw materials	water	wood pulp
	chlorophyll	acid
	carbon dioxide	
Energy	sunlight	coal
Product		paper
	wood, fruit, etc.	
Waste	oxygen	sulfur dioxide

5. *Discuss where the analogy breaks down.* The teacher explains that photosynthesis, unlike a factory, produces a waste product that is useful to humans—oxygen.

6. *Draw conclusions.* Photosynthesis is similar to a factory, but it is far more efficient and rarely creates environmental problems (except in the case of weeds!).

EXTENSIONS AND VARIATIONS

Thinking with analogies can be modified in many ways. Here are just a few:

- At the conclusion of a unit, suggest several analogies and ask students to critique them. (Which analogies work and which don't?)
- When students have worked with analogies for a while, ask them to suggest their own analogies for selected concepts.
- Ask students to engage in reciprocal teaching, explaining a new concept to another group by means of an analogy.

READ MORE ABOUT IT
♦ ♦ ♦

Glynn, S. (1989). The teaching with analogies model. In K. D. Muth (Ed.), *Children's comprehension of text: Research into practice* (pp. 185–204). Newark, DE: International Reading Association.

Glynn, S. (1995). Conceptual bridges: Using analogies to explain scientific concepts. *The Science Teacher, 62*(9), 25–27.

Glynn, S. (1996). Teaching with analogies: Building on the science textbook. *The Reading Teacher, 49,* 490–492.

Readence, John E., Moore, David W., and Rickelman, Robert J. (2000). *Prereading activities for content area reading and learning* (3rd ed.). Newark, DE: International Reading Association.

Charting New Territory

◆ ◆ ◆

Forgive the pun in the chapter title above, but charting is one of the simplest and most effective ways of helping children learn from nonfiction text. A chart is any arrangement of information in rows and columns. When students engage in charting, they first locate information in a print source, decide where it belongs in the chart, and place it there. Research clearly shows that activities that cause students to translate information from one form to another help them better understand the content. Charting is such an activity.

SOME ADVANTAGES OF CHARTING

Charting permits flexibility in planning. It can be used as a purpose-setting activity *prior* to reading, or it can become a *post*reading activity. It lends itself to collaborative interaction among students, and it can provide the basis of class discussions as the contents are reviewed as a group. It also leaves students with something succinct to study as they prepare for tests. Best of all (at least from the perspective of most students), charts require very little writing. They're long on thinking and short on tedium. The basic thinking skill entailed in charting is *categorization*, one of the most important cognitive processes in any subject area. Charting has a hidden benefit as well. It helps students understand how charts work, and this understanding aids them in interpreting charts and even in creating their own as they write.

SOME TYPES OF CHARTS

As long as it has rows and columns, it's a chart! You needn't be concerned about whether you're using a particular kind of chart. The only important consideration is whether the chart makes sense to students—whether it helps them think through the content of a reading selection. Here are a few types that might help get you started. Keep in mind, however, that the best plan is often to fashion your own chart based on the nature of the content.

T-Charts

The T-chart is probably the simplest type of chart. It resembles a large lower-case *t* and requires students to categorize information into either of two columns. It's great for stressing comparisons and contrasts. It's also a good way to begin charting with your students. With T-charts, you provide the two column headings. The students do the rest. (An example appears on p. 136.)

Tables

A table is a chart in which most of the information is in the form of numbers. Tables are useful in virtually all subject areas. Being able to interpret tabular data is an essential literacy skill, and constructing simple tables from nonfiction selections is a good starting point.

Two-Column Charts

A very simple chart is one that arranges information in two columns. The first provides a topic, the second a corresponding fact or figure. Part of a two-column chart on Florida, for example, might look like this:

Population	about 15 million
Area	about 60,000 square miles
State flower	orange blossom
State bird	mockingbird

(Notice that a chart can combine numbers with verbal information.)

Multiple-Column Charts

Simply by adding columns, you can dramatically increase the amount and variety of information a chart contains.

Feature Analysis Charts

A special type of multiple-column chart involves semantic feature analysis. The left-hand column includes members of a particular category. The columns to the right are devoted to features that each category member may or may not have. The interior of a feature analysis chart is completed with plusses and zeros, depending on whether a member possesses or lacks a particular feature. (The letter *s* can be used in cases where a member *sometimes* possesses a certain feature.) Feature analysis is the most thoroughly researched form of charting. The results give it an unqualified "thumbs-up" as one of the most effective instructional activities available. (See feature analysis charts in Section 3, pp. 37–44.)

INSTRUCTIONAL TIPS FOR CHARTING

Here are some suggestions for integrating charts more effectively into your instruction.

- ◆ Look for examples of charts in reading selections and make them the basis of discussion.
- ◆ Pose questions that require students to locate information in a published chart.
- ◆ Start your students on the road to constructing their own charts by using simple ones. Progress gradually to more complex charts.
- ◆ Fill in part of the chart yourself as an example of what the chart requires the students to do.
- ◆ Make a transparency of the chart and display it during a class discussion. Complete it with a marker as you call on individual students for input.

Name _____ Date _____

From *Help for Struggling Readers* by Michael C. McKenna. Copyright 2002 by The Guilford Press. Permission to photocopy this page is granted to purchasers of this book for personal use only (see copyright page for details).

Name _____ Date _____

_____	_____	_____
_____	_____	_____
_____	_____	_____
_____	_____	_____
_____	_____	_____
_____	_____	_____
_____	_____	_____
_____	_____	_____
_____	_____	_____
_____	_____	_____
_____	_____	_____
_____	_____	_____
_____	_____	_____
_____	_____	_____
_____	_____	_____
_____	_____	_____

From *Help for Struggling Readers* by Michael C. McKenna. Copyright 2002 by The Guilford Press. Permission to photocopy this page is granted to purchasers of this book for personal use only (see copyright page for details).

Guided Notes

◆ ◆ ◆

Guided notes (Lazarus, 1988) are one form of reading, or study, guide. They provide an incomplete, skeletal version of text notes to be completed as the student reads. As such, they are designed to lead a student through a reading assignment and provide assistance in processing and recording information. At the same time, they model what good notes should look like and actively engage students in the process of producing them. Their value lies both in the thinking a student must do to create them and in the review aid they provide when complete.

PROCEDURE

The goal is to produce a skeleton outline of text content. If a teacher has already prepared lecture notes over a chapter or other reading selection, the first step is to highlight main ideas and key words. These become the basis of the handout eventually given to the student, with sufficient space for the student's written additions. If the teacher must start from scratch, the material must be read and analyzed while notes are taken using an abbreviated, informal outline format. Lazarus has recommended the following considerations:

1. Include at least the main ideas and key terms on the student copies.
2. Provide guided notes for everyone in the class.
3. Use a consistent format that closely parallels the lecture, reading assignment, and/or content to be learned.
4. Show complete copies of the guided notes on transparencies.
5. Periodically evaluate the students' guided notes.
6. Train the students to use the guided notes for review.

A "review tally" can be placed at the top of the form. This is a simple grid that allows the student to place a checkmark in one of its squares each time the notes are reviewed.

VARIATIONS

Since guided notes are a form of reading guide, other types of guides might be employed as variants. However, many reading guide formats are not designed with reading-disabled students in mind and tend to pose questions and add comments that might in themselves present reading difficulties rather than model what good notes should resemble. For a review of alternative reading guide formats, see pp. 132–143 and also McKenna and Robinson (2002).

ADVANTAGES

Guided notes actively engage students in reading and thinking. They produce an excellent tool for review, and their worth has been demonstrated with less-able students.

LIMITATIONS

This technique emphasizes relatively low levels of comprehension. Producing the student forms is time-consuming for teachers, and completing them might become tedious for students over time.

VALIDATION

Given the extensive validation of reading and study guides in general (e.g., see Alvermann and Swafford, 1989), it is not surprising that guided notes have produced good results in the few research trials undertaken to date with reading disabled populations. Lazarus (1991, 1996) found that the technique improved the scores of these students on chapter tests in regular science and social studies classes. While more research is necessary, guided notes seem to be off to a good start.

READ MORE ABOUT IT
◆ ◆ ◆

Alvermann, D. E., & Swafford, J. (1989). Do content area strategies have a research base? *Journal of Reading, 32,* 388–394.

Lazarus, B. D. (1988). Using guided notes to aid learning disabled students in secondary mainstream settings. *The Pointer, 33,* 32–36.

Lazarus, B. D. (1991). Guided notes, review, and achievement of learning disabled adolescents in secondary mainstream settings. *Education and Treatment of Children, 14,* 112–128.

Lazarus, B. D. (1996). Flexible skeletons: Guided notes for adolescents with mild disabilities. *Teaching Exceptional Children, 28*(3), 36–40.

McKenna, M. C., & Robinson, R. D. (2002). *Teaching through text: A content literacy approach to content area reading* (3rd ed.). New York: Longman.

Reading Guides

◆ ◆ ◆

A reading guide is a list of questions and other tasks to which a child must respond while reading. Reading guides are sometimes called study guides or content literacy guides. Their purpose is to focus a child's attention on key ideas during reading and to provide a tool for later review and discussion. Guides differ from postreading questions in that comprehension is affected as the student reads, not afterward.

There is no formula for constructing a reading guide, no right or wrong way. Each guide is unique in that a teacher must first decide what it is important for students to grasp and then construct tasks for helping them do so. These tasks might include:

- Questions to be answered
- Charts to be completed
- Diagrams to be constructed
- Pictures to be drawn
- Responses to be written

There is really no limit to the ways such tasks can be created and interwoven, and there is certainly an element of creativity in constructing a good reading guide! The following steps might be helpful:

- Read the selection carefully.
- Decide which ideas and facts are important to know.
- Create tasks that help students attain this knowledge.
- Include a variety of tasks, not just questions.
- Aim for simple wordings.
- Leave plenty of space for children to write.
- Arrange the tasks sequentially.
- Include page numbers and/or subheads.
- Where appropriate, include comprehension aids.

Reading guides have numerous advantages, as teachers who use them regularly will attest:

♦ They improve comprehension by focusing students' attention on important aspects of content.
♦ They make reading an active rather than a passive process.
♦ They cause students to translate the material into their own words, phrases, and sentences.
♦ They are a means of integrating reading and writing.
♦ They produce a useful tool for review.
♦ They provide a blueprint for postreading discussion and give students a valuable discussion aid.
♦ They model strategic, purposeful reading.
♦ They model effective notetaking.

Of course, reading guides have disadvantages as well. They take time to create, they require paper, and they have to be copied. These drawbacks can be daunting, but using guides on a trial basis will soon persuade teachers that the advantages are worth it!

Here are some tips for using reading guides effectively.

1. Model their use. Students must be instructed in what is expected of them as they complete a guide.
2. Monitor closely. Troubleshoot as students read and complete the guides in class.
3. Tie the guides to discussion. Ask students to place their completed guides on their desks prior to a discussion, and use the guides to anchor that discussion.
4. Encourage students to use the guides to review. Since guides provide a form of notes over what the students have read, they can be used as a valuable aid in reviewing for tests or in writing about the selection.
5. Revise if necessary. Be alert to weaknesses in the guides you create. Word process changes so that an improved guide is ready the next time you teach the same selection.
6. Give guides time to work. The full impact of reading guides may not become evident until they have been used routinely for a few months. Once their use has become a part of in-class reading, students will complete them knowledgeably and may even complain when they are not provided!

EXAMPLE

On pp. 135–136, a sample guide appears, covering a short subsection of a science textbook (see p. 99). Note the variety of tasks, the ample space provided, and the advice to skip part of the reading.

READ MORE ABOUT IT

◆ ◆ ◆

McKenna, Michael C., and Robinson, Richard D. (2002). *Teaching through text: A content literacy approach to content area reading* (3rd ed.). New York: Longman.

Wood, Karen D., Lapp, Diane, and Flood, James. (1992). *Guiding readers through text: A review of study guides*. Newark, DE: International Reading Association.

Pluto

Reading Guide

Section A
p. 99
"Pluto"

How cold is Pluto

Since 1999, which planet has been farthest from the sun?

_____ Neptune

_____ Pluto

_____ Venus

Calendars and clocks would be very different on Pluto!
Fill in these times:

Length of Pluto's Day _____ Earth Days (round it off)

Length of Pluto's Year _____ Earth Years (round it off)

p. 99
"You're How Old?"

Skip this sidebar.

Do you think there's life on Pluto?
Check one:

_____ Most likely, there is.

_____ Most likely, there is not.

What evidence do you have for your opinion?
List your reasons in the chart below:

Evidence of Life	Evidence of NO Life

Anticipation Guides

◆ ◆ ◆

The anticipation guide is a special type of reading guide useful with nonfiction selections that may challenge students' preconceived ideas about certain topics. Such a guide consists of a series of statements about the material covered by the selection. Students read the statements prior to the selection and indicate whether they agree or disagree with each. The teacher and the class openly discuss the statements, but the teacher refrains from suggesting responses. The rationale of the anticipation guide is simple: The statements activate appropriate prior knowledge, and a student's responses provide hypotheses to be tested through reading. The purpose for reading is to test their hypotheses.

When well constructed, anticipation guides have the potential to stimulate interest, not only because they can create controversy but also because they help students clear up misconceptions and accommodate new information that may be at odds with their previous thinking. Duffelmeyer (1994) offers four steps for creating an effective anticipation guide:

Step 1. Identify the major ideas presented in the material to be read.
Step 2. Consider what beliefs your students are likely to have.
Step 3. Create statements that target those beliefs.
Step 4. Arrange the statements in a manner that requires either a positive or negative response.

On the following pages are two examples of anticipation guides, one that follows these steps and one that doesn't (Duffelmeyer, 1994). Take a moment to contrast the two. Remember, it's vital that you write statements that students can react to in advance and that do not exceed their prior knowledge.

Anticipation guides are not well suited to every nonfiction selection. When the material touches on common misconceptions, however, be ready to create one as a change of pace. Once you've finished the guide, follow these steps in using it:

Step 1. Mention the topic of the selection and provide some background without "giving away" the correct responses to the guide.

Step 2. Tell the students to read each statement in advance and to place a check mark in the "Agree" or "Disagree" column.

Step 3. After they read, have students return to the guide. Class discussion should focus on which check marks need to be changed and why.

EXAMPLE 1: AN ANTICIPATION GUIDE WITH POOR STATEMENTS

Directions: Read each statement below. If you believe that a statement is *true*, place a *check mark* in the "Agree" column. If you believe that a statement is false, place a *check mark* in the "Disagree" column. Be ready to explain your choice.

Agree Disagree

{ }   { }   1. A varve has two sediment layers, one coarse and the other fine.
(*Flaw*: insufficient background knowledge)

{ }   { }   2. The velocity of streams and rivers remains the same year round.
(*Flaw*: subordinate idea)

{ }   { }   3. If you cut down a tree, you will see that it has rings.
(*Flaw*: common knowledge)

{ }   { }   4. All carbon atoms have the same weight.
(*Flaw*: insufficient background knowledge)

{ }   { }   5. The carbon-14 method can date objects that are one million years old.
(*Flaw*: insufficient background knowledge)

{ }   { }   6. A Geiger counter measures radioactive atoms.
(*Flaw*: subordinate idea)

{ }   { }   7. The half-life of uranium is longer than the half-life of carbon-14.
(*Flaw*: insufficient background knowledge)

EXAMPLE 2: AN ANTICIPATION GUIDE WITH GOOD STATEMENTS

Directions: Read each statement below. If you believe that a statement is *true*, place a *check mark* in the "Agree" column. If you believe that a statement is false, place a *check mark* in the "Disagree" column. Be ready to explain your choice.

Agree   Disagree

{ }   { }   1. In order to measure time you need a clock or a calendar.

{ }   { }   2. Most of the mud, rocks, and other natural material on the bottom of a lake was there before the lake was formed.

{ }   { }   3. The age of one tree can be used to tell the age of some other tree.

{ }   { }   4. After something dies, it decays very quickly.

{ }   { }   5. Determining how old an ancient object is involves a lot of guesswork.

{ }   { }   6. Scientists can tell how old something is even if it was never alive.

{ }   { }   7. The older a rock is, the harder it is to determine its age.

On the next few pages, you will find a reproducible anticipation guide and an interesting expository selection about bananas. Note how the guide statements target possible misconceptions or facts that seem counterintuitive. Use this example with your students if you find it appropriate.

READ MORE ABOUT IT

◆ ◆ ◆

Duffelmeyer, Frederick A. (1994). Effective anticipation guide statements for learning from expository prose. *Journal of Reading, 37,* 452–457.

McKenna, Michael C., and Robinson, Richard D. (2001). *Teaching through text: A content literacy approach to content area reading* (3rd ed.). New York: Longman.

Tierney, Robert J., and Readence, John E. (2000). *Reading strategies and practices: A compendium* (5th ed.). Boston: Allyn & Bacon.

Extended Anticipation Guide for Partners or Small Groups

Directions (before): Take turns reading each statement in Part I with your Partner. If you believe the statement is *true*, put a checkmark in the "Agree" column. If you believe it is *false*, checkmark the "Disagree" column. Be ready to explain your answer to each other and the class.

Agree   Disagree

_____ _____ 1. Bananas are berries.

_____ _____ 2. Bananas grow on trees.

_____ _____ 3. Bananas are the second most important commercial fruit sold in the United States.

_____ _____ 4. In addition to being an excellent source of potassium, vitamins A and C, and quick energy, bananas are a major source of protein.

_____ _____ 5. The banana is at its best eating condition when the bright yellow peeling is flecked with brown specks.

_____ _____ 6. More bananas come from Ecuador than any other country.

_____ _____ 7. The botanical name for banana, Musa Sapientum, derives from the legend that sages in India sat under banana trees during times of meditation.

From *Help for Struggling Readers* by Michael C. McKenna. Copyright 2002 by The Guilford Press. Permission to photocopy this page is granted to purchasers of this book for personal use only (see copyright page for details).

The Truth About Bananas

Scientific Name
Family: Musaceae
Genus: *Musa*
Species: *Musa* acuminata (common banana)
         Musa paradisica (plantain banana)

Food Value
Water: 75.7%
Protein: 1.1 g
Fat: 0.2 g
Carbohydrates: 22.2 g

Food Energy:
Approximately 1 calorie per gram
Vitamin A: 190 IU
Thiamine (B_1): 0.05 mg
Riboflavin (B_2): 0.06 mg
Phosphorous: 26 mg
Potassium: 370 mg
Vitamin C: 10 mg
Niacin: .7 mg
Calcium: 8 mg
Iron: .7 mg
Sodium: 1 mg

Which of these statements are true?

a. The banana is a berry.

b. Bananas grow on trees.

c. Pound for pound, bananas are the most widely sold fruit in the United States.

d. Bananas are highly nutritious and easily digestible.

There are over 100 varieties of bananas!

The Banana Plant

You may be surprised to learn that bananas are berries! A berry is a simple fruit having a skin surrounding one or more seeds in a fleshy pulp. Botanists classify grapes, tomatoes, currants, and bananas as berries.

Bananas grow on a tropical plant that is not a tree—it has no trunk. Bananas are gigantic herbs that spring from underground stems. What appears to be the trunk is a false stem formed by tightly wrapped leaf sheaths that grows to a height of three or more meters. From the top, 10-20 large oblong to elliptical-shaped leaves fan out. It takes 5-18 months to grow the one stalk of bananas it bears. Bananas on the stalk point upward. After harvesting, the plant is cut down and the underground rootstock produces new shoots for the next plant.

MATH + SCIENCE: A SOLUTION © 1987 AIMS Education Foundation

The HISTORY of Bananas

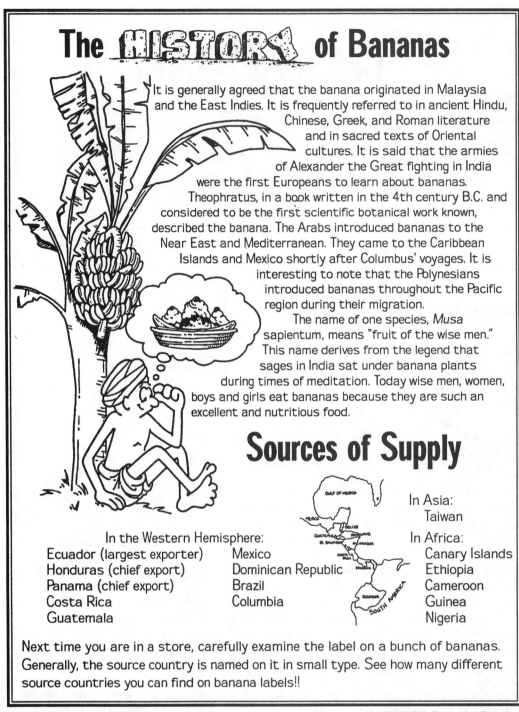

It is generally agreed that the banana originated in Malaysia and the East Indies. It is frequently referred to in ancient Hindu, Chinese, Greek, and Roman literature and in sacred texts of Oriental cultures. It is said that the armies of Alexander the Great fighting in India were the first Europeans to learn about bananas. Theophratus, in a book written in the 4th century B.C. and considered to be the first scientific botanical work known, described the banana. The Arabs introduced bananas to the Near East and Mediterranean. They came to the Caribbean Islands and Mexico shortly after Columbus' voyages. It is interesting to note that the Polynesians introduced bananas throughout the Pacific region during their migration.

The name of one species, *Musa sapientum*, means "fruit of the wise men." This name derives from the legend that sages in India sat under banana plants during times of meditation. Today wise men, women, boys and girls eat bananas because they are such an excellent and nutritious food.

Sources of Supply

In the Western Hemisphere:
Ecuador (largest exporter)   Mexico
Honduras (chief export)   Dominican Republic
Panama (chief export)   Brazil
Costa Rica   Columbia
Guatemala

In Asia:
Taiwan

In Africa:
Canary Islands
Ethiopia
Cameroon
Guinea
Nigeria

Next time you are in a store, carefully examine the label on a bunch of bananas. Generally, the source country is named on it in small type. See how many different source countries you can find on banana labels!!

MATH + SCIENCE: A SOLUTION

© 1987 AIMS Education Foundation

The Banana as Food

Pound for pound, bananas are the most widely sold fruit in the United States. They are the most important of all commercial fruits, close to the combined production of all citrus fruits.

Bananas are an excellent food source of potassium, vitamins A & C, and quick energy. They are low in protein and fat. They are an excellent between-meal snack and one of the most easily digested and nutritious natural foods. A medium-size banana has about 125-130 calories, or about one calorie per gram. Bananas are recommended for low-fat, low-sodium diets.

Bananas come with their own wrapping, ready to go into lunch boxes. They are tasty sliced on breakfast cereals, in fruit salads, and gelatin desserts. Bananas are used in the preparation of flavoring. Vacuum dehydration yields banana crystals, a light-brown powder used in ice cream, bakery products and milk-based beverages.

"Tree-ripened" would not make good advertising for bananas. If allowed to ripen on the plant they are starchy, mealy, or rotten and therefore inedible. They are sent to market green and are ripened in air-tight rooms with controlled humidity and temperature. These conditions permit nearly all of the starch to be converted into sugar for good taste. The banana is at its best eating condition when the bright yellow peeling is flecked with brown specks, known as "sugar specks." Look for plump, well-filled fruit.

A plantain is a cooking variety of banana that is larger than our common banana. It is a staple food in the tropics. Plantains are starchy when green and take the place of potatoes. Plantain chips are the Latin-American equivalent of our potato chips!

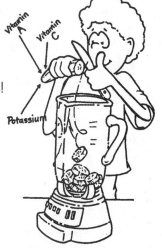

Vitamin A
Vitamin C
Potassium

Easy-to-Make Banana Shake

1 whole peeled banana
1 cup milk
1 dash of nutmeg (to taste)
Combine ingredients and
　　　blend until smooth.

Reciprocal Teaching

♦ ♦ ♦

Many of the struggling readers in the upper elementary and middle grades have developed adequate decoding skills. What they lack are strategies for comprehending nonfiction material. Reciprocal teaching, introduced by Palincsar and Brown in 1982, is an instructional technique through which students work in small groups, together applying comprehension strategies to a new reading selection. These strategies include predicting, clarifying, questioning, and summarizing. In order for reciprocal teaching to work, the teacher must spend some time explaining these four strategies so that the students can apply them to new material. Research suggests that this is time well spent. Let's briefly examine each of them.

The students begin by examining the reading selection and *predicting* what it seems likely to be about. To do so they consider subtitles, pictures, boldfaced terminology, and graphic aids. Some students may not be used to predicting, so starting with simple examples, such as pictures and picture books, may be necessary.

New content material may well contain concepts and ideas that are not entirely clear while students are reading. In *clarifying*, they focus on words, ideas, and even pronunciations that may require further explanation. Others in the group may be able to help, as can the teacher. The important thing is that they realize where the problems lie.

Students are asked to engage in *questioning* once they have read each portion of a selection. They are encouraged to ask questions at a variety of comprehension levels. Training in Question–Answer Relationships (QARs) can help. Other members of the collaborative group will attempt to answer these questions as they are asked.

Once the students are finished asking and answering their own questions, they begin *summarizing* what they have read and discussed. One option is to have students co-author a written summary, but other possibilities include producing an informal outline of new material, creating a semantic map, or simply identifying the most important ideas and terminology introduced in the selection.

These four strategies are used by proficient readers whenever they encounter new content material. Such readers form predictions about what the text will be about, though these predictions may not always be formally worded. Then, as they read, they attempt to clarify the meanings of new terms and reflect on difficult ideas before moving on. They often form questions as they read and do their best to answer them. When they finish a selection, they consider the major points it has taught them and the overall significance it may have. For the proficient reader, all of these strategies are applied internally and independently. They form a kind of dialogue, through which good readers attempt to monitor their own comprehension in order to ensure understanding. Struggling readers frequently lack this internal "conversation," and their comprehension suffers as a result. Reciprocal teaching is a means of fostering these healthy mental habits.

PREPARING STUDENTS FOR RECIPROCAL TEACHING

It is important to take nothing for granted in getting students ready for reciprocal teaching experiences. Palincsar and Brown (1986) have suggested several steps for accomplishing this goal.

1. *Instruction.* Carefully explain and define each of the four strategies (predicting, clarifying, questioning, summarizing). These are abstract terms, so do not take understanding for granted.

2. *Modeling.* On the basis of selections that are familiar to the students, illustrate how to apply the strategies. Encourage the students to contribute to the teacher-led examples by generating questions and predictions of their own and also by contributing to summaries.

3. *Guided practice.* As new selections are introduced, gradually shift the responsibility for applying the strategies to the students. Call upon them in the course of the dialogue to play an increasing role in making predictions, seeking clarification, asking questions, and creating summaries. Monitor the students' efforts, providing feedback and praise where needed.

CONDUCTING A RECIPROCAL TEACHING LESSON

Once the students have had some experience in applying the four strategies in guided settings, it is time to conduct a reciprocal teaching lesson from start to finish. In describing a typical lesson, we'll draw on the experience of Claire Smith and Joanne Pelton, seventh-grade teachers at Winder–Barrow Middle School in Georgia. These two colleagues have refined the technique of reciprocal teaching with their own struggling seventh-grade readers and report phenomenal success in improving both comprehension ability and content learning.

Students should be assigned to groups of four to six without regard to reading proficiency. Students with behavioral problems may need to be separated from one another or even given different assignments during reciprocal teaching time. The selection to be read is introduced to the students in much the same way as any reading assignment. The teacher builds background by briefly introducing the topic and linking it to previous content. The teacher stops short, however, of introducing the material in great detail (as might be the case in Listen–Read–Discuss, for example) because of the fact that the students will be assisting one another during the processes of questioning and clarifying.

A reminder of the steps in the reciprocal teaching process is posted so that the students can refer to it as necessary. The first box on p. 147 shows how Joanne Pelton outlines her expectations for each of the strategies that the students will undertake during reciprocal teaching.

Within each group, one of the students serves as "teacher" and is responsible for keeping the group on task as it moves from one strategy to the next and from one page to the next. This does not mean that the "teacher" conducts instruction, however. The role of "teacher" is rotated among the group members from one reciprocal teaching lesson to the next. The composition of the groups remains relatively stable over time unless in the teacher's judgment (the classroom teacher, that is!) a better mix can be established by transferring one or more students.

The teacher's expectations for a particular reciprocal teaching lesson are made clear at the beginning by placing them on a transparency or on the board and by checking to be sure that the students clearly understand what is required. The second box on p. 147, contains an example of how Joanne Pelton sets purposes for a lesson on dolphins, based on an issue of *Current Science*. Notice that she pointed students toward a culminating activity, in this case the creation of a poster that allowed them an opportunity to apply what they learned from the selection. You might also want to display the chart on p. 148, which was developed by Claire Smith to remind students of the four components.

After the students begin, the teacher monitors their activity by "hobnobbing" from one group to another. It may be necessary to provide prompts, ask questions, suggest clarifications, or take other actions in order to keep a group on task. As the lesson proceeds, Claire Smith describes what she calls "The Wave." The groups will naturally reach different strategies at different times, and one group may be relatively quiet (for instance, during the reading phase) while others are engaged in active discussion. This constructive noise then moves on to another group.

ADVANTAGES OF RECIPROCAL TEACHING

Reciprocal teaching not only accomplishes its purpose of fostering strategic reading on the part of struggling readers, it is highly motivational and appropriately based on social interaction. Claire Smith and Joanne Pelton have even used reciprocal teaching as a reward. It is clearly an instructional approach worthy of regular use. Best of all, the reading selections are your own subject-matter materials, so that reciprocal teaching does not require time that is set aside from content instruction.

READ MORE ABOUT IT

◆ ◆ ◆

Marzano, Robert J., Pickering, Debra J., and Pollock, Jane E. (2001). *Classroom instruction that works: Research-based strategies for increasing student achievement.* Alexandria, VA: ASCD.

Palinscar, A. S., and Brown, A. L. (1984). Reciprocal teaching of comprehension fostering and comprehension monitoring activities. *Cognition and Instruction, 1*(2), 117–175.

Rosenshine, Barak, and Meister, C. C. (1994). Reciprocal teaching: A review of the research. *Review of Educational Research, 64,* 479–530.

Steps in a Reciprocal Teaching Lesson

(As worded by Joanne Pelton and posted for her seventh graders)

Predict
> Use clues from pictures, the title, and subtitles.
> Each student makes a prediction.

Read Aloud
> One paragraph per student until you have finished a page.
> Go on to the next step.

Clarify
> Focus on an idea, word, or pronunciation you need help on.
> Make sure everyone in the group understands before going on.

Question
> Ask questions that can be answered from the page you just read.
> Ask questions that may require inferring.
> Ask questions that may require evaluation.

Summarize
> When you are finished clarifying and questioning, summarize the page. You may do this by outlining, making a word web, or listing the most important points.

Sample Directions for a Reciprocal Teaching Lesson

1. Reciprocal teach the article on pages 4, 5, 6, and 7.

2. As a group, design a poster that you, as Beach Rangers, would post at a beach to educate the public about dolphins. Use the blank sheet of paper I'll give you to get your ideas together, and then have your "teacher" pick up the markers and poster board from Mrs. Pelton.

   (*Hint*: List or illustrate characteristics of dolphins that the public may need to know. But remember, you are out of a job if people are not warned or if they are scared off.)

RECIPROCAL TEACHING

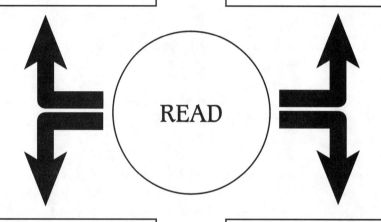

PREDICT	QUESTION
Make an educated guess about what will happen in the passage.	*Ask a question about the reading*

READ

CLARIFY	SUMMARIZE
Define words that are hard to understand	*Tell about what was read.*

From *Help for Struggling Readers* by Michael C. McKenna. Copyright 2002 by The Guilford Press. Permission to photocopy this page is granted to purchasers of this book for personal use only (see copyright page for details). This chart was created by Claire Smith and is reprinted here with her permission.

Guided Reading in Textual Settings

◆ ◆ ◆

Many struggling readers have had little or no experience in learning from nonfiction. When asked to read a selection independently, their response may be avoidance or outright refusal. More often, they will attempt the task without a clear idea of what to do. Guided Reading in Textual Settings (GRITS) is a practical strategy for involving students in such learning, with continuous support from the teacher. Developed by Lisa Davis, a Georgia middle school teacher, it combines several research-based instructional techniques into a single comprehensive teaching strategy. GRITS includes:

- Chapter walk-throughs
- Reading guides
- Think-alouds
- Graphic organizers
- Charting
- Prediction and other focusing techniques
- Partitioning a reading selection into short segments

GRITS takes little for granted. The teacher assumes (1) that students have little background knowledge of the topic they will read about, (2) that they are not very good at setting their own strategic purposes as they read nonfiction, (3) that they are not used to thinking actively about new content, and (4) that they are easily frustrated, distracted, or bored. Does this sound like your students? It is undoubtedly true of a great many struggling readers in the upper elementary and middle grades. Here's how GRITS works:

Step 1. Read the material in advance, looking for terms, expressions, references, and ideas that are likely to create difficulties for students. Newly introduced technical terms will be adequately explained in the text, of course, but there may be other points at which the author assumes too much prior knowledge on the part of students. Try to anticipate these points, and think of questions and comments that might assist students.

Step 2. Prepare a reading guide. Be certain to include graphic organizers and simple charts. Also, provide opportunities within the guide for students to illustrate concepts and ideas that may be best understood visually. (Students must, of course, already be familiar with reading guides.)

Step 3. Conduct a chapter walk-through prior to the actual reading of the text by students. Walk the students through the material, focusing first on pictures and other graphics. Ask them to predict what each picture portrays before they read the caption; then contrast the caption with their conjecture. Next, consider the subheadings and point out the organizational structure of the text that the subheadings suggest.

Step 4. Build background for the selection. Begin by talking about any introductory matter the text selection contains. This could include a list of technical terms, guiding questions, etc. Then read the first paragraph aloud to the class. Use this paragraph to build background by discussing terminology, raising questions, and making predictions.

Step 5. Ask the students to read the next paragraph silently. Monitor and provide assistance if needed. Then call on someone to read the same paragraph aloud. Ask questions that help students make connections with prior knowledge or arrive at inferences. Use think-alouds where needed to model how students should process challenging new content. (e.g., "Here's what I thought at first . . ., but now . . ." or "That doesn't seem to make sense. Let's keep reading to see . . . "). Try to suggest analogies that might help students relate unfamiliar and abstract content to ideas that are already well understood.

Step 6. Ask students to complete the portion of the reading guide for that paragraph. Monitor and troubleshoot as they work.

Step 7. Proceed through the selection paragraph by paragraph, following the same procedures (silent reading, oral rereading, discussion, and guide). Some material may be structured such that a section, or perhaps two or three paragraphs, can be read before following the procedures. The question of exactly how much material to cover before pausing to discuss or to direct students to complete a portion of the reading guide is text dependent. The teacher should make this decision during the preparation phase of the lesson.

Step 8. Conduct a postreading discussion of the entire selection, anchored in (but not entirely limited to) the completed reading guide.

GRITS may strike some teachers as dull. Indeed, reading a textbook is seldom very exciting. There are two compelling justifications for the GRITS approach, however. First, textbooks present important course content and provide a powerful and available teaching tool. Second, far too many readers in the upper elementary and middle grades lack the background knowledge and strategic know-how to read textbooks without considerable teacher support. GRITS addresses the twin goals of acquiring content and becoming a better reader of nonfiction. Most of us will agree that, when confronted with a choice between dessert versus meat and potatoes, children will generally opt for dessert. GRITS is meat and potatoes.

Remember, too, that many of the elements of this approach provide opportunities to enliven the material. By posing inferential questions, calling for predictions, offering analogies to students' experiences, and providing opportunities to draw, for example, teachers can bring the material to life and make it both accessible and enjoyable.

EXAMPLE

A complete example of GRITS would require a full textbook chapter! The illustration offered here focuses on how a teacher might present two short paragraphs that form one subsection of a chapter on weather and climate. The passage comes from a sixth-grade geography text.*

> As you learned in Chapter 1, the earth's tilt and rotation cause different regions to receive different amounts of heat and light from the sun. The sun's direct rays fall year-round at low latitudes near the Equator. This area—known as the tropics—lies mainly between the Tropic of Cancer and the Tropic of Capricorn. If you lived in the tropics, you would almost always enjoy a hot climate, unless you lived at a high elevation where temperatures are cooler.
> Outside the tropics the sun is never directly overhead. In the high-latitude regions around the north and south poles, darkness descends for six months each year. There the sun's rays hit the earth indirectly at a slant. Thus, climates in these regions are always cool or cold even in midsummer. (p. 41)

Remember that in GRITS the teacher has already built some background by examining the first paragraph of the chapter with the students, by conducting a chapter walk-through, and by briefly discussing key terms listed at the beginning of the chapter. Thereafter, as the students discuss each successive paragraph, background is further extended.

When the class reaches the first of the two paragraphs above, the teacher asks the

Source: Boehm, Richard G., Armstrong, David G., and Hunkins, Francis P. (2000). *Geography: The World and Its People* (Vol. 1). New York: McGraw-Hill.

students to read the paragraph silently. One student, a volunteer, then reads the paragraph aloud. The teacher refers the students to the map they studied in Chapter 1. A classroom globe becomes useful as a three-dimensional prop for illustrating how the sun's rays fall upon regions differently. Anticipating uncertainty about the phrase "low latitudes," the teacher explains it by referring to the map. The class locates the Tropic of Cancer and the Tropic of Capricorn on their copies of the map. Before moving to the next paragraph, the teacher calls students' attention to the guide. "Is there a question here you can answer now?" the teacher asks. Someone responds by identifying and reciting such a question.

This process is repeated for the second paragraph, though there are opportunities for variety. "Can you imagine what it would be like if the sun didn't come up for six months?" the teacher might ask, just after one of the students has read the sentence aloud. Such a question is provocative because it relates content to students' lives, making an abstract idea seem more relevant. A think-aloud might be appropriate here as well. "It says, 'the sun's rays hit the earth indirectly at a slant,' " the teacher observes. "I wonder what that really means. I know what *slanted* means. Hmm, maybe we could make a sketch." The teacher might even darken the room for a moment and shine a flashlight at the globe.

Since the two paragraphs together make up a brief subsection, the teacher discourages the students from responding to the guides until they have processed both paragraphs. Then time is provided for the students to update the guides by responding to the questions they encounter there or to perform the other tasks required. The teacher monitors to ensure that the students have completed this portion of the guide properly. The process is then repeated for the next paragraph or subsection.

Summary Writing

◆ ◆ ◆

"**A** summary," Judith Irvin has remarked, "is a collection of main ideas." It is also more than that, however, for it "involves integrating the ideas into a coherent whole" (1998, p. 170). Writing a summary is therefore both a reading and a writing task.

Research has clearly shown that writing summaries improves comprehension of the material that has been read and enhances comprehension ability generally. These are impressive claims! One reason summary writing is so effective is that it compels students to transform content into their own words and expressions. Doing so requires active thought. Another reason is that students must make repeated judgments about the relative importance of ideas. They must separate main ideas from details and string the main ideas together into a coherent account.

No wonder writing summaries is among the most challenging tasks any student can face! This is why it is important to provide careful instruction, rich in examples and support. The following suggestions are offered with respect to the ability of your students and their experience in summarizing.

BEGINNING STAGES

- Begin by discussing newspaper headlines. A headline is always a main idea, complete with a subject and verb. Select stories related to a particular content area if you wish.
- Progress to having students write headlines, given the lead paragraph of a news story.
- Practice oral summaries of brief passages, such as a chapter subsection. Model them first.
- Move to having students write summaries of brief passages as a postreading activity.

153

LATER STAGES

♦ Have students write main idea statements for chapter subsections, then string them together, editing for coherence. Students could work collaboratively, each responsible for one of the sentences and the entire team for the finished product.

♦ Encourage the use of graphic organizers as an aid in writing summaries.

♦ Use chapter summaries found in texts as models.

APPROACH 1: HIERARCHICAL SUMMARIES

Barbara Taylor (1986) developed a method of assisting middle schoolers in writing coherent summaries. Her five steps include the following:

Step 1. Read only the subheadings of a chapter.
Step 2. List the subheadings on paper.
Step 3. Read the material.
Step 4. Convert each subheading into a main idea sentence.
Step 5. For each main idea sentence, add from one to three sentences giving supporting details.

Example of Writing a Hierarchical Summary

Subheadings listed (Step 2):

> Legislative Branch
> Executive Branch
> Judicial Branch
> Checks and Balances

Subheadings converted to main idea sentences (Step 4):

> The Legislative Branch is responsible for passing laws.
> The Executive Branch is responsible for enforcing the laws.
> The Judicial Branch is responsible for interpreting laws . Checks and balances are ways of making sure no branch becomes too powerful.

Addition of detail sentences (Step 5):

The Legislative Branch is responsible for passing laws. Each law begins as a bill. The legislators must vote on a bill to see whether it will become a law.

The Executive Branch is responsible for enforcing the laws. The police are part of the executive branch. Also, agencies like the IRS, FBI, and EPA are part of this branch. They make sure laws are enforced.

The Judicial Branch is responsible for interpreting laws. The court system makes up this branch. When cases come to court, judges decide how laws should be interpreted. Sometimes laws are thrown out.

Checks and balances are ways of making sure no branch gets to be too powerful. For example, the Executive Branch checks the Judicial Branch by appointing judges. The Legislative Branch could check the Executive Branch by overriding a veto. The Judicial Branch might check the Legislative Branch by declaring a law unconstitutional.

APPROACH 2: GRASP

David Hayes (1989) developed an effective group strategy for teaching summary writing. He called it the Guided Reading and Summarizing Procedure (GRASP). His technique is similar to List–Group–Label, used for vocabulary reinforcement.

Step 1. After the students have read a section of text, ask them to turn their books face down. Ask them to recall whatever they can from the material. Record their input in a list on the board or on a transparency.

Step 2. Allow the students to return to the text and to locate more information and to make corrections.

Step 3. With student participation, rearrange the information into categories.

Step 4. Help the students write a topic sentence for each category and detailing sentences that support it.

Step 5. Engage the students in revising the summary to make it more coherent.

APPROACH 3: WHO-WANTS-BUT-SO FOR FICTION SUMMARIES

Summarizing fiction differs from nonfiction summarizing because the structure of the material is so different. A good starting point is the Who-Wants-But-So approach applied to a short story. Students first write a sentence that identifies the main character. They next tell what this person is trying to accomplish along with the obstacles standing in the way. Last, they specify the outcome. The example that follows applies this approach to a common folktale.

Example of Who-Wants-But-So: Jack and the Beanstalk

Who: Jack is a poor and foolish boy who lives with his mother.
Wants: He wants to sell their cow . . .
But: but trades her instead for some magic beans.
So: A beanstalk grows into the sky and Jack climbs it. He discovers a giant's castle and robs the giant. He is nearly killed trying to escape.

Who-Wants-But-So is good for starters, but it does not work very well with all stories. True, most fiction does center around a protagonist who must overcome obstacles to achieve a goal. Our example of Jack and the Beanstalk stretches this format a bit since Jack created his own obstacles. After all, he could have sold the cow as his mother asked him to do, but that would not have made for a very good story!

ADDITIONAL SUGGESTIONS

Vacca and Vacca (2002) offer additional ideas for helping students write effective summaries:

- ◆ Compare a student summary with one you have written yourself. Make sure there is no possibility of embarrassment by (1) using a summary written in a previous year and (2) not revealing the identity of the student writer.
- ◆ Provide the class with three summaries, one that is good, another that is fair, and a third that is poor. Involve the students in rating and discussing the three.
- ◆ Place students in pairs or small groups and ask that they read their summaries to each other. They can provide each other with feedback that is used to revise.

READ MORE ABOUT IT
◆ ◆ ◆

Hayes, David A. (1989). Helping students grasp the knack of writing summaries. *Journal of Reading, 33*, 96–101.

Irvin, Judith L. (1998). *Reading and the middle school student* (2nd ed.). Boston: Allyn & Bacon.

Taylor, Barbara M. (1986). Teaching middle grade students to summarize content textbook material. In J. F. Baumann (Ed.), *Teaching main idea comprehension* (pp. 195–209). Newark, DE: International Reading Association.

Vacca, Richard T., and Vacca, Jo Anne L. (2002). *Content area reading: literacy and learning across the curriculum* (7th ed.). New York: Longman.

Cloze Venns

◆ ◆ ◆

Venn diagrams can be combined with the cloze procedure to stimulate inferential thinking, even when there is only a very brief amount of text to be read by students. In cloze exercises, one or more words are replaced with blanks so that students must infer them from context. In a Cloze Venn, only one blank is used. By making certain that the context offers multiple clues, you can create logical puzzles that are really quite engaging. These steps may help organize the process:

Step 1. Write a sentence or two containing a single blank. Make sure the context contains two clues as to an acceptable word for the blank. There should be more than one acceptable word.

Step 2. Place the text and an empty Venn on the board or transparency and help the students process the information. Begin by extracting the clues and labeling each of two circles that you draw with one clue.

Step 3. Try to suggest at least one word for every section of the Venn so that students can contrast right and wrong answers.

Step 4. When and if you feel your students are ready, proceed from two-circle to three-circle Venns. (These will require three clues in the text you write, of course.)

You may be able to use the samples on the following pages, which are designed either for transparency masters or duplicated worksheets. All of the texts are quite simple. Some lead to two-circle Venns, some to three-.

EXAMPLE

Even struggling readers can relate to exercises as simple as this one, which rewards reasoning rather than proficiency at extended reading.

My pet is a _____. He has four legs.

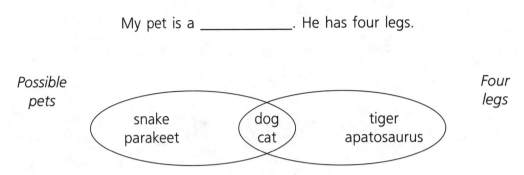

TEACHING VARIATION

Once students are familiar with this activity, try asking them to write their own contexts. You may need to edit them before sharing them with the class.

Thirsty Girl

Sue was a strange girl. She refused to drink anything that was not brown in color. That is why she drank so much _____.

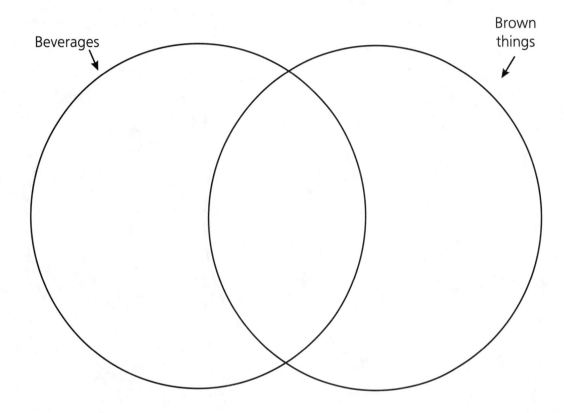

From *Help for Struggling Readers* by Michael C. McKenna. Copyright 2002 by The Guilford Press. Permission to photocopy this page is granted to purchasers of this book for personal use only (see copyright page for details).

The Fruit Stand

Ted stopped at the fruit stand and bought one _____. He wanted to plant a tree.

Kinds of fruit

Things you can eat that grow on trees

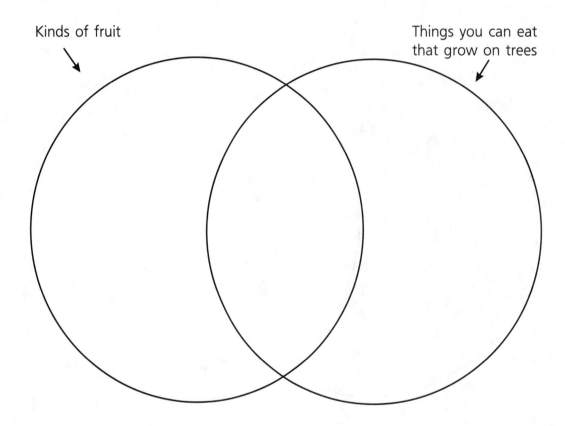

From *Help for Struggling Readers* by Michael C. McKenna. Copyright 2002 by The Guilford Press. Permission to photocopy this page is granted to purchasers of this book for personal use only (see copyright page for details).

Bill and Sue

Sue is related to Bill. She is his _____.

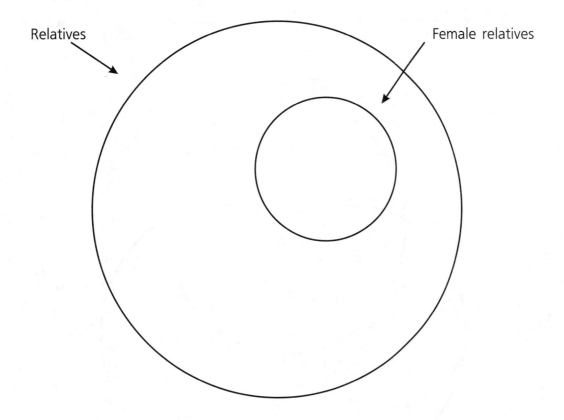

From *Help for Struggling Readers* by Michael C. McKenna. Copyright 2002 by The Guilford Press. Permission to photocopy this page is granted to purchasers of this book for personal use only (see copyright page for details).

Baby Names

A woman had just had a baby boy. She was trying to think of a name. She liked simple names of only one syllable. She also liked names beginning with the letter *j*. She finally decided to call her son _____.

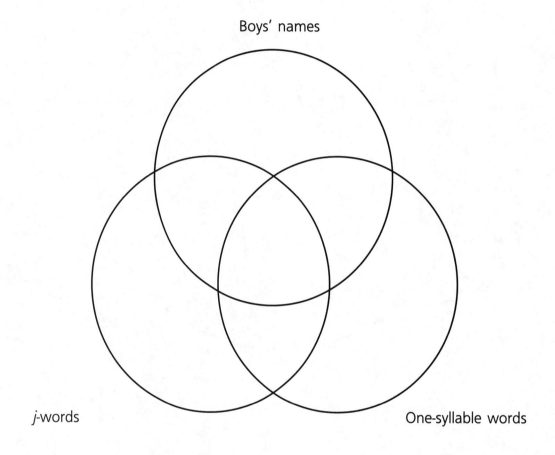

Boys' names

j-words

One-syllable words

From *Help for Struggling Readers* by Michael C. McKenna. Copyright 2002 by The Guilford Press. Permission to photocopy this page is granted to purchasers of this book for personal use only (see copyright page for details).

Bug Girl

She frowned when the _____ flew by her head. She hated bugs!

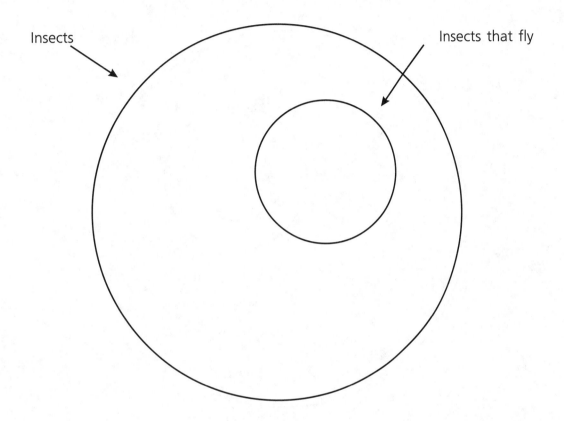

Insects

Insects that fly

From *Help for Struggling Readers* by Michael C. McKenna. Copyright 2002 by The Guilford Press. Permission to photocopy this page is granted to purchasers of this book for personal use only (see copyright page for details).

The New Tree

Although he liked fruit trees, he decided to plant one _____ in his yard.

Trees

Fruit trees

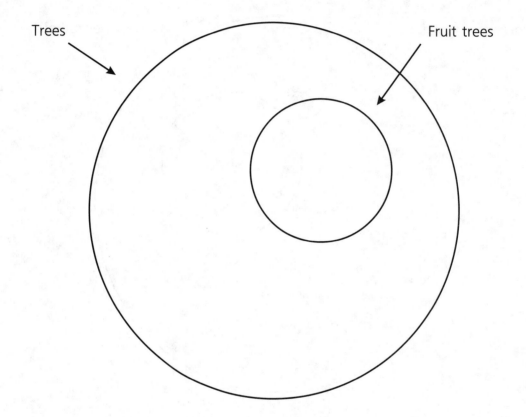

From *Help for Struggling Readers* by Michael C. McKenna. Copyright 2002 by The Guilford Press. Permission to photocopy this page is granted to purchasers of this book for personal use only (see copyright page for details).

Green Food

Green was Tyrone's favorite color. That's why he ate _____ whenever he wanted a vegetable.

Vegetables

Green vegetables

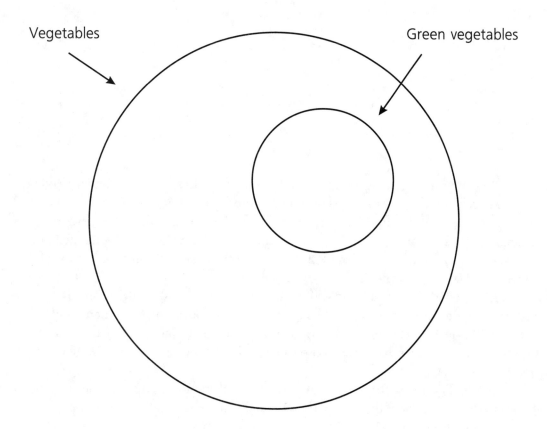

From *Help for Struggling Readers* by Michael C. McKenna. Copyright 2002 by The Guilford Press. Permission to photocopy this page is granted to purchasers of this book for personal use only (see copyright page for details).

Riddles

◆ ◆ ◆

Riddles offer an engaging sponge activity, one that stimulates inferential reading comprehension. They're also short and require little reading time. Putting one on the board as students file in from recess or another class can be both challenging and focusing. I suggest one rule, however: that the answer not be blurted out by the first person who solves it. Students who think they've found the answer might be asked to come forward and write it down where only you can see.

Keep in mind that not all riddles lend themselves to logical solution. This is especially true of riddles with puns as answers. These can be frustrating for students and will soon lead to the expectation that the riddles you choose are jokes rather than puzzles and therefore can't be solved. So choose well. Real riddles can be solved through logic and insight.

Some riddles are poetic in form and expose students to verse while they present their puzzle. A number of these appear on the following pages in the form of black-line masters (answers are on p. 178). Try them as sponge work.

Riddle I

I am blood, though never red,
and those I'm found in never bled.
I move beneath their rugged skin
and carry life to leaf and limb.

From *Help for Struggling Readers* by Michael C. McKenna. Copyright 2002 by The Guilford Press. Permission to photocopy this page is granted to purchasers of this book for personal use only (see copyright page for details).

Riddle II

Unique among beasts, I hold humans in thrall,
noblest of creates and greatest of all
in form I am equine with flowing white mane,
confusing to those who have pondered in vain
on seeing my beard and my spiraling spear
rising in triumph twixt left and right ear—
now think, gentle reader, and tell me my name.

From *Help for Struggling Readers* by Michael C. McKenna. Copyright 2002 by The Guilford Press. Permission to photocopy this page is granted to purchasers of this book for personal use only (see copyright page for details).

Riddle III

I am a frown without a face,
a lazy lone parenthesis;
I am an arc above a shoal,
and bowed abode of toll and troll.

From *Help for Struggling Readers* by Michael C. McKenna. Copyright 2002 by The Guilford Press. Permission to photocopy this page is granted to purchasers of this book for personal use only (see copyright page for details).

Riddle IV

I am a roof, though some complain
I give no shelter from the rain.
I am a bowl placed upside down
And cover mountaintop and town.
I am a window, giving light,
Yet home to darkness and to night.

From *Help for Struggling Readers* by Michael C. McKenna. Copyright 2002 by The Guilford Press. Permission to photocopy this page is granted to purchasers of this book for personal use only (see copyright page for details).

Riddle V

He clasps the crag with crooked hands;
Close to the sun in lonely lands,
Ring'd with the azure world, he stands.

The wrinkled sea beneath him crawls;
He watches from his mountain walls,
And like a thunderbolt he falls.

From *Help for Struggling Readers* by Michael C. McKenna (2002). This riddle is a poem by Alfred, Lord Tennyson.

Riddle VI

This thing all things devours;
Birds, beasts, trees, flowers;
Gnaws iron, bites steel;
Grinds hard stones to meal;
Slays king, ruins town,
And beats high mountain down.

From *Help for Struggling Readers* by Michael C. McKenna. Copyright 2002 by The Guilford Press.
Permission to photocopy this page is granted to purchasers of this book for personal use only (see copyright
page for details).

Riddle VII

Upon four legs it walks at dawn,
But two of them, by noon, are gone,
And when the sun is in the west,
It finds that then three legs are best.

From *Help for Struggling Readers* by Michael C. McKenna. Copyright 2002 by The Guilford Press. Permission to photocopy this page is granted to purchasers of this book for personal use only (see copyright page for details).

Riddle VIII

I kiss the earth and touch the sky,
Yet neither lips nor hands have I.
I harm no creature, great or small,
Unless, of course, I chance to fall.
I am so strong I'll never tire,
But fear I termite, axe, and fire.

From *Help for Struggling Readers* by Michael C. McKenna. Copyright 2002 by The Guilford Press. Permission to photocopy this page is granted to purchasers of this book for personal use only (see copyright page for details).

Riddle IX

Why is a raven like a writing-desk?

From *Help for Struggling Readers* by Michael C. McKenna (2002). From *Alice's Adventures in Wonderland*, by Lewis Carroll, illustration by Sir John Tenniel.

Riddle X

'Tis never seen, though not invisible.
This thing and you are indivisible.
You could not think of it without it.
You use it even if you doubt it.
What is it then? Why, *think* about it!

From *Help for Struggling Readers* by Michael C. McKenna. Copyright 2002 by The Guilford Press. Permission to photocopy this page is granted to purchasers of this book for personal use only (see copyright page for details).

Riddle XI

A narrow Fellow in the Grass
Occasionally rides—
You may have met Him—did you not
His notice sudden is—

The Grass divides as with a comb—
A spotted shaft is seen—
And then it closes at your feet
And opens further on—

From *Help for Struggling Readers* by Michael C. McKenna (2002). This riddle is a poem by Emily Dickinson.

ANSWERS TO RIDDLES

- ◆ *Riddle I*: Tree sap (Michael McKenna, unpublished).
- • *Riddle II*: A unicorn (Michael McKenna, unpublished). (This one's an acrostic!)
- • *Riddle III*: A bridge (Michael McKenna, *Cricket*, September 1998).
- • *Riddle IV*: The sky (Michael McKenna, unpublished).
- • *Riddle V*: An eagle. (This is actually the title of a poem by Tennyson. When the title is removed, the poem becomes a riddle!)
- • *Riddle VI*: Time. (This riddle was solved accidentally by Bilbo Baggins in J. R. R. Tolkien's *The Hobbit*.)
- • *Riddle VII*: Man. (This is the riddle of the Sphynx, set to verse. According to ancient Greek legend, the Egyptian Sphynx was once a living creature—a giant beast with the head of a woman and the body of a lion. Any traveler unlucky enough to venture past her was asked this riddle: "What walks on four legs in the morning, two legs at midday, and three legs in the evening?" Anyone failing to give the answer was destroyed. Eventually, however, Oedipus happened by and answered, "Man." Man crawls on all fours as an infant, walks upright in maturity, and needs a cane in old age. When the Sphynx heard this, she was turned to stone and has remained that way ever since!)
- • *Riddle VIII*: A tree (Michael McKenna, unpublished).
- • *Riddle IX*: This is the famous riddle posed by the Mad Hatter in the children's classic, *Alice's Adventures in Wonderland*. Alice cannot answer it, and the Mad Hatter—maddeningly!—doesn't bother giving the solution. People have speculated for more than a century now, and it might be fun to see what your students can come up with. Martin Gardner, who edited *The Annotated Alice*, gives a few solutions that have been offered over the years. Among them:

> Because it can produce a few notes, tho' they are very flat (Lewis Carroll's own later suggestion).
>
> Because Poe wrote on both (Sam Loyd).
>
> Because there is a *b* in *both*. (This answer would probably have delighted Carroll; it was proposed by a Dr. Rieu, in a letter quoted by Graham Edwards, of Penguin Books.)

- ◆ *Riddle X*: The brain (Michael McKenna, unpublished). (Note that *mind* will not work as an answer since the mind is in fact invisible.)
- • *Riddle XI*: These are the opening lines of a poem by Emily Dickinson. The poem is untitled, but most folks agree she's writing about a snake. You may want to use the entire poem, which is referred to only as No. 986.

SOME COMMERCIAL SOURCES OF RIDDLES

Cricket magazine is an excellent source of riddles. In addition, there are many books of riddles to choose from. Here are just a few.

1. Liza Jemstone. (1996). *World's Greatest Riddle Collection* (Joy Books). Grades 2 and up. ISBN 1-886197-00-8.

2. Katy Hull and Lisa Eisenberg. (1993). *Snaky Riddles* (Puffin Books). Pre-kindergarten–grade 3. ISBN 0140545883.

3. Darwin A. Hindman. (1963). *1,800 Riddles and Enigmas and Conundrums* (Dover). Grade 4 and up. ISBN 0-486-21059-6.

4. Briggs LeBaron. (1972). *Riddles and Rhymes* (Golden Press). ISBN 0-8490-0957-X.

Puzzlers

♦ ♦ ♦

On the following pages you will find brief descriptions of events that pose problems in logic (answers are on p. 187). Your students may very well find them perplexing. The idea is to make them think—something they may not be used to doing as they read!

Each puzzler is simply written so that deficits in prior knowledge and decoding will not get in the way. You may still wish to read them aloud, however, as students follow along, if you think it necessary.

The passages are designed as sponge activities and are presented in a format that will allow you to create either transparencies or hard copies. It is important to establish some ground rules before using them, however. Be sure your students know there is a problem to solve, and make it clear that no one is to blurt out the answer. When you discuss each puzzler after the students have read it, they may well offer alternative answers. Use constructive criticism as you discuss their suggestions.

The Car Wreck

A man and his son were in a very bad car accident. The father was not hurt, but the boy was near death. He was rushed to a hospital. Luckily, a famous surgeon was on duty. The surgeon worked for many hours to save the child's life. After the operation, there was good news: the boy would live!

A nurse said to the surgeon, "You were great! I've never seen you operate so well."

The surgeon smiled and said to the nurse, "I had an extra reason today. That boy is my own son, you know."

Is there something about this story that doesn't make sense?

From *Help for Struggling Readers* by Michael C. McKenna. Copyright 2002 by The Guilford Press. Permission to photocopy this page is granted to purchasers of this book for personal use only (see copyright page for details).

Bob's Cafe

Jim and Sue had been married to one another only a month when they went to a new restaurant called Bob's Cafe. Jim had never been to Bob's Cafe before. That is why he was surprised to see his wife there.

Does this little story make sense? Can you think of a way to make it make sense?

From *Help for Struggling Readers* by Michael C. McKenna. Copyright 2002 by The Guilford Press. Permission to photocopy this page is granted to purchasers of this book for personal use only (see copyright page for details).

The Case of the Missing Bodies

When the policeman opened the door of the house, he knew exactly what had happened. The bodies were gone, but there was still lots of evidence. On the couch the killer sat looking at the policeman. The killer did not seem at all afraid.

The policeman frowned. He knew the killer was guilty, but he did not draw his gun. Instead, he walked to the couch and sat down next to the killer. Then he picked the killer up, placed him on his lap, and scratched his ears. The policeman looked at the broken aquarium and the big wet place on the floor. He shook his head.

"Felix," he said to his cat, "What am I ever going to do with you?"

Did this story have you fooled? Which sentence helped you figure out what really happened? Oh, yes, and just what were those missing bodies?

From *Help for Struggling Readers* by Michael C. McKenna. Copyright 2002 by The Guilford Press. Permission to photocopy this page is granted to purchasers of this book for personal use only (see copyright page for details).

A Nutty Question

A squirrel is on the trunk of a tree. You are standing on the other side of the tree. You cannot see the squirrel. You are not even sure a squirrel is there.

Slowly, you walk around the tree. The squirrel does not want you to see it. It moves around the trunk so that the trunk is always in between. In a minute you come back to where you started. You still have not seen the squirrel.

Have you walked around the squirrel?

From *Help for Struggling Readers* by Michael C. McKenna. Copyright 2002 by The Guilford Press. Permission to photocopy this page is granted to purchasers of this book for personal use only (see copyright page for details).

Frog on a Log

A frog is sitting on the end of a log. It jumps exactly half way across. It then jumps again, this time traveling half the remaining distance. It keeps jumping in this way, each time going just half the distance to the other end of the log.

Will the frog ever get to the other end of the log?

From *Help for Struggling Readers* by Michael C. McKenna. Copyright 2002 by The Guilford Press. Permission to photocopy this page is granted to purchasers of this book for personal use only (see copyright page for details).

Heavy Birds

A large truck is filled with birds. You cannot see them from the outside because the truck has walls and a ceiling. The truck driver stops at a weigh station. He is told that his truck is too heavy for the highway.

"Just a minute," the driver says. "I can fix that."

Standing beside his truck, the driver beats on the walls with a stick. This frightens the birds and makes them fly around inside the truck.

Will this really make the truck weigh less?

From *Help for Struggling Readers* by Michael C. McKenna. Copyright 2002 by The Guilford Press. Permission to photocopy this page is granted to purchasers of this book for personal use only (see copyright page for details).

ANSWERS TO PUZZLERS

♦ *The Car Wreck*: This story is really about gender stereotypes. Most children will think of a "famous surgeon" as a man. If the surgeon were the boy's mother, however, the story would make perfect sense.

♦ *Bob's Cafe*: This story paraphrases the famous opening of Ben Travers's novel, *Mischief*, published in the 1920s. The writer never says that Jim and his wife go to the cafe *together*. Most readers assume they did because of their notions regarding newlyweds and because of the way they take certain things for granted as they read.

♦ *The Case of the Missing Bodies*: All of the students will be fooled, whether they admit it or not! Their prior knowledge of policemen and killers will mislead them. Most will realize they've been had when they get to the sentence, "Then he picked the killer up, placed him on his lap, and scratched his ears." The "missing bodies" were the tropical fish that had been eaten.

♦ *A Nutty Question*: Yes, the child will walk around the squirrel. Whether the squirrel is seen by the child makes no difference. To prove it, draw a diagram of the child, the squirrel, and the tree as seen from above. Trace the squirrel's path along the outer edge of the tree. Then draw the child's path, making a circle that completely encompasses the tree and the squirrel.

♦ *Frog on a Log*: No, the frog will never get to the other end of the log because there will always be a small part of the log remaining. Some students may think that because the frog is always making progress toward the other end that it will get there eventually. Not so.

♦ *Heavy Birds*: Yes, the truck will weigh less because the birds are not adding their own weight to that of the truck while they are in flight. That is, as long as they are flying about inside, they are not pressing down on the truck and the scales beneath it.

20 More Ideas for Inferential Comprehension

◆ ◆ ◆

1. *Treasure Hunts*. Hide a small "treasure" somewhere in your classroom or elsewhere in the school. Then hide clues at strategic points and provide groups of students with the first clue. Their task is to work together to infer the location of the next clue. Different groups could follow different routes to the same treasure.

2. *Mini-Mysteries*. Present students with a short description of a crime scene containing the clues necessary for its solution. Use the chalkboard or a transparency. Good sources include *Two-Minute Mysteries* (1991) and *Still More Two-Minute Mysteries* (1995) by Donald J. Sobol (Apple) and *Five-Minute Mysteries* (and various sequels) by Kenneth J. Weber (1989, Running Press).

3. *Story Problems*. (Math) Solving mathematical story problems always requires inferential comprehension. Their solution provides a good opportunity to focus on two core areas at the same time! An interesting variation is to have students write story problems for others to solve.

4. *Aphorisms*. Old sayings, such as "a stitch in time saves nine," are frequently couched in metaphorical language. This saying, for instance, isn't really about sewing. Its true meaning has to be inferred. Having students interpret the meanings of aphorisms is a good exercise in inferential comprehension.

5. *Picture Interpretation*. Show students a picture portraying people in action. Invite discussion of what preceding events (not depicted) must have occurred in order to result in the situation in the picture. Then direct the discussion toward what may occur after the point portrayed in the picture. Norman Rockwell's paintings are an excellent source.

6. *Twenty Questions*. The traditional game in which one person thinks of an object while others ask a series of yes–no questions in an effort to guess the object is a superb

opportunity to develop inferential comprehension skills. One class member can be "it" while others attempt to guess through questioning. Teams could also be formed. Discussing with students the relative effectiveness of some of their questioning strategies should be incorporated into this technique.

7. *Headline Writing*. Provide students with copies of news stories without the headlines. Their task is to write a suitable headline for each story. The ability to do so requires students to infer the main idea of the story.

8. *Sequencing Comics*. Clip two- and three-frame comic strips from the daily paper and then cut apart the frames. Rearrange the frames in random order, and then have students determine from the pictures and dialogue the proper original sequence.

9. *Secret Codes*. Have one student or a group of students develop a secret code by associating each of the 26 letters of the alphabet with another letter. A message is then encoded and provided to a second student or group of students who must decipher it, based on word length, word arrangement, frequency of letter use, etc.

10. *Elaboration*. As a story is being read, pause frequently and ask students to elaborate on the scene being developed by the author. For example, students can describe settings, characters, and incidents as they imagine them to be, filling in details that the author has omitted. Research shows clearly that effective readers elaborate mentally. Teachers should therefore encourage this activity.

11. *Syllogisms*. Present students with simple syllogisms to encourage straightforward inferences, or have them construct their own. For example:

a. Los Angeles is in California.
b. California is in the United States.
c. Therefore, Los Angeles is in the United States.

An interesting variation, once the idea of the syllogism has been grasped, is to leave out one of the three statements and have students infer it. Begin by leaving out the last statement.

12. *Cloze Exercises*. Present students with sentences in which one word has been deleted and replaced with a blank. Make sure that the context of the missing word contains enough information to generate a reasonable guess. This exercise benefits not only inferential comprehension but word recognition as well. For example:

The kids were afraid of my pet _____.

13. *Maze Exercises*. An easier alternative to cloze is to provide students with sentences in which, at a certain point, three words are presented, typed one atop another. Only one word makes sense based on context. For example:

	try.
The squirrel hid his nuts in a	tree
	truth.

Maze experiences can be made to stress higher-order skills by using options that are all semantically acceptable. The task in this case is to select the one best word on some other basis, such as its poetic qualities. In the following example from Shakespeare, all the choices are sensible but one is inspired:

                    tone
The iron tooth   of midnight hath told twelve.*
              tongue

14. *Writing Morals.* After the class has discussed a story, ask class members to compose a "moral," in the way Aesop's fables were written. Constructing morals emphasizes main ideas.

15. *Writing Blurbs.* After a student has finished a book, rather than writing a formal book report, the student might be asked to write a blurb instead—that is, a brief, tempting description of what the book is about. Main idea comprehension skills are stressed in this exercise. A blurb is really a type of summary. Summary writing is one of the best comprehension activities children can undertake, and blurbs make writing them fun.

16. *Analogies.* Present students with incomplete analogies, for which they must infer the missing component. For example:

black : white :: hot : _____

Note that the blank can replace any of the four elements, although you should begin by replacing the fourth. As students attempt to solve analogies, encourage them to infer the basis on which the analogy is made. In the example above, this basis is opposites.

17. *Hypothesizing.* Before students begin a reading assignment (or before they continue with an assignment they've already begun), have them formulate a hypothesis about what will happen next. This is a good way to develop the important inferential skill of predicting outcomes. The purpose for their reading then becomes the testing of the hypothesis. (This activity is the basis of Russell Stauffer's Directed Reading–Thinking Activity, or DR-TA.) (See pp. 88–89.)

18. *Causal Triads.* Show students groups of three simple sentences. Two of the sentences represent a cause-and-effect relationship while the third sentence is irrelevant. For example:

a. Sue found a wounded rabbit in the woods.
b. Sue enjoys playing soccer.
c. Sue decided to keep the rabbit as a pet.

Students must first eliminate the irrelevant fact and then decide which of the two remaining facts is the cause and which is the effect. When students catch on, progress to

*The right choice is *tongue*, which creates a pun on *toll* and *tell*. Did you infer correctly?

three statements that depict a sequence of causes. The students must now arrange the sentences in causal order. (All three are relevant.) Write them on the board in random order and have students unscramble them on the basis of cause. For example:

    a. John decided to mow lawns.
    b. John needed money.
    c. John advertised in the paper.

This is a good exercise for developing the ability to infer cause-and-effect relationships.

19. *Story Starters.* The traditional idea of providing students with a brief beginning to a story and asking them to complete it is often used to develop creative capacities. However, it can also be used to develop inferential comprehension skills when students' continuations are judged on the basis of how reasonably they mesh with the starter itself. That is, can the continuation be defended? Is it logical? This activity could be done in a group setting in which each student contributes a single sentence to a story and also provides a justification for why that continuation makes sense.

20. *Writing Inferential Questions.* Have students write inferential questions about a selection they have read. Allow the class to judge whether the questions can be answered on the basis of the selection. This activity can also be a purpose-setting device. That is, you can ask students to write one or more inferential questions *as they read*.

SECTION 7

◆ ◆ ◆

Suggested Professional Resources

GENERAL

Allington, Richard L., and Cunningham, Patricia M. (2001). *Schools that work: Where all children read and write* (2nd ed.). Boston: Allyn & Bacon. ISBN 0-801-33246-X. [Call 800-666-9433]

Cunningham, Patricia M., and Allington, Richard L. (1999). *Classrooms that work: They can all read and write* (2nd ed.). New York: HarperCollins. ISBN 0-321-01339-5. [Call 800-782-2665]

Davidson, Judith, and Koppenhaver, David. (1993). *Adolescent literacy: What works and why* (2nd ed.). New York: Garland. ISBN 0-8153-0920-1. [Call 800-821-8312]

Gambrell, Linda B., Morrow, Leslie M., Neuman, Susan B., and Pressley, Michael. (Eds.). (1999). *Best practices in literacy instruction*. New York: Guilford Press. ISBN 1-57230-442-1. [Call 800-365-7006]

Marzano, Robert J., Pickering, Debra J., and Pollock, Jane E. (2001). *Classroom instruction that works: Research-based strategies for increasing student achievement*. Alexandria, VA: Association for Supervision and Curriculum Development. ISBN 0-87120-504-1. [Call 800-933-2723]

McKenna, Michael C., and Robinson, Richard D. (2002). *Teaching through text: A content literacy approach to content area reading* (3rd ed.). New York: Longman. ISBN 0-8013-3263-X. [Call 800-282-0693]

Robinson, Richard D., McKenna, Michael C., and Wedman, Judy M. (Eds.). (2000). *Issues and trends in literacy instruction* (2nd ed). Boston: Allyn & Bacon. ISBN 0-205-29651-3. [Call 800-666-9433]

U.S. Department of Education. (1999). *Start early, finish strong: How to help every child become a reader*. Washington, DC: U.S. Department of Education. [Full text available at www.ed.gov/pubs/edpubs.html; to order a print copy, call toll free 877-4ED-PUBS]

WORD RECOGNITION

Bear, Donald R., Invernizzi, Marcia, Templeton, Shane, and Johnston, Francine. (2000). *Words their way: Word study for phonics, vocabulary, and spelling instruction* (2nd ed.). Upper Saddle River, NJ: Prentice Hall. ISBN: 0-130-21339-X. [Call 800-643-5506]

Cunningham, Patricia M. (2000). *Phonics They Use: Words for Reading and Writing* (3rd ed.). New York: Longman. ISBN: 0-321-02055-3. [Call 800-282-0693]

Cunningham, Patricia M., and Hall, Dottie P. (1994). *Making words*. Parsippany, NJ: Good Apple. [More than one volume now available] ISBN 0-86653-806-2. [Call 800-421-5565]

Cunningham, Patricia M., and Hall, Dottie P. (1994). *Making big words*. Parsippany, NJ: Good Apple. [More than one volume now available] ISBN 0-86653-807-0. [Call 800-421-5565]

Cunningham, Patricia M., and Hall, Dottie P. (1998). *Month-by-month phonics for upper grades*. Greensboro, NC: Carson-Dellosa. ISBN 0-88724-473-4. [Call 800-321-0943]

Fry, Edward B., Kress, Jacqueline E., and Fountoukidis, Dona L. (2000). *The reading teacher's book of lists* (4th ed.). Upper Saddle River, NJ: Prentice Hall. ISBN: 0-13-028185-9. [Call 800-643-5506; give the operator the following "key code": E1001-A1(3)]

VOCABULARY AND COMPREHENSION

Allington, Richard L. (Ed.). (1998). *Teaching struggling readers*. Newark, DE: International Reading Association. ISBN 0-87207-183-9. [Order online at http://www.reading.org, or call 302-731-1600]

Beck, Isabel L., McKeown, Margaret G., Hamilton, Rebecca L., and Kucan, Linda. (1997). *Questioning the author: An approach for enhancing student engagement with text*. Newark, DE: International Reading Association. ISBN 0-87207-242-8. [Order online at http://www.reading.org, or call 302-731-1600]

Bromley, Karen D. (1996). *Webbing with literature: Creating story maps with children's books* (2nd ed.). Boston: Allyn & Bacon. ISBN 0-205-16975-9. [Call 800-666-9433]

Bromley, Karen, Irwin-De Vitis, Linda, and Modlo, Marcia. (1995). *Graphic organizers: Visual strategies for active learning*. New York: Scholastic. ISBN 0-590-48928-3.

Doolittle, John H. (1991). *Dr. DooRiddles*. Pacific Grove, CA: Critical Thinking Books and Software. [Progressive series of riddle books, each with its own ISBN]. [Call 800-458-4849]

Heimlich, Joan E., and Pittelman, Susan D. (1986). *Semantic mapping: Classroom Applications*. Newark, DE: International Reading Association. ISBN 0-87207-230-4. [Order online at http://www.reading.org, or call 302-731-1600]

Moore, David W., Alvermann, Donna E., and Hinchman, Kathleen A. (2000). *Struggling adolescent readers: A collection of teaching strategies*. Newark, DE: International Reading Association. ISBN 0-87207-272-X. [Order online at http://www.reading.org, or call 302-731-1600]

Nagy, William E. (1988). *Teaching vocabulary to improve reading comprehension*. Newark, DE: International Reading Association. ISBN 0-87207-151-0. [Order online at http://www.reading.org, or call 302-731-1600]

Pittelman, Susan D., Heimlich, Joan E., Berglund, Roberta L., and French, Michael P. (1991). *Semantic feature analysis: Classroom applications*. Newark, DE: International Reading Association. ISBN 0-87207-235-5. [Order online at http://www.reading.org, or call 302-731-1600]

Readence, John E., Moore, David W., and Rickelman, Robert J. (2000). *Prereading activities for content area reading and learning* (3rd ed.). Newark, DE: International Reading Association. ISBN 0-87207-261-4. [Order online at http://www.reading.org, or call 302-731-1600]

Sloane, Paul. (1992). *Lateral thinking puzzlers*. New York: Sterling. [One of several in a series by Sloane] ISBN 0-8069-8227-6. [Call 800-367-9692]

Spear-Swerling, Louise, and Sternberg, Robert J. (1996). *Off track: When poor readers become learning disabled*. Boulder, CO: Westview Press. ISBN: 0-8133-8757-4. [Call 800-386-5656]

Stahl, Steven A. (1999). *Vocabulary development: From research to practice* (Vol. 2). Cambridge, MA: Brookline Books. ISBN 1-57129-072-9. [Call 800-666-BOOK]

Tierney, Robert J., and Readence, John E. (2000). *Reading strategies and practices: A compendium* (5th ed.). Boston: Allyn & Bacon. ISBN 0-205-29808-7. [Call 800-666-9433]

Wood, Karen D., Lapp, Diane, and Flood, James. (1992). *Guiding readers through text: A review of study guides*. Newark, DE: International Reading Association. ISBN 0-87207-374-2. [Order online at http://www.reading.org, or call 302-731-1600]

MOTIVATION AND ATTITUDE

Baker, Linda, Dreher, Mariam J., and Guthrie, John T. (Eds.). (2000). *Engaging young readers: Promoting achievement and motivation*. New York: Guilford Press. ISBN 1-57230-535-5. [Call 800-365-7006]

Cramer, Eugene H., and Castle, Marietta. (Eds.). (1994). *Fostering the love of reading : The affective domain in reading education*. Newark, DE: International Reading Association. ISBN: 0-87207-125-1. [Order online at http://www.reading.org, or call 302-731-1600]

Evans, Karen S. (2001). *Literature discussion groups in the intermediate grades: Dilemmas and possibilities*. Newark, DE: International Reading Association. ISBN: 0-87207-293-2. [Order online at http://www.reading.org, or call 302-731-1600]

Gambrell, Linda B., and Almasi, Janice F. (1996). *Lively discussions!: Fostering engaged reading*. Newark, DE: International Reading Association. ISBN: 0-87207-147-2. [Order online at http://www.reading.org, or call 302-731-1600]

Grindler, Martha C., Stratton, Beverly D., and McKenna, Michael C. (1997). *The right book, the right time: Helping children cope*. Boston: Allyn & Bacon. ISBN 0-205-17272-5. [Call 800-666-9433]

Phelan, Patricia. (Ed.). (1996). *High interest—easy reading: An annotated booklist for middle school and senior high school* (7th ed.). Urbana, IL: National Council of Teachers of English. ISBN 0-8141-2098-9. [Call 800-369-6283]

Snow, Catherine, and Verhoeven, Ludo. (Eds.). (2001). *Literacy and motivation: Reading engagement in individuals and groups*. Hillsdale, NJ: Erlbaum. ISBN: 0-8058-3193-2.

Stoll, Donald R. (Ed.). (1997). *Magazines for kids and teens* (rev. ed.). Newark, DE: International Reading Association. ISBN 0-87207-243-6. [Order online at http://www.reading.org, or call 302-731-1600]

Trelease, Jim. (1995). *The read-aloud handbook* (4th ed.). New York: Penguin. ISBN: 0-1404-6971-0. [Call 800-788-6262]

Zahler, Kathy A. (1997). *50 simple things you can do to raise a child who loves to read*. New York: Macmillan. ISBN 0-02-861765-7. [Call 800-262-4729]

Index

Accelerated Reader, 31
Analogies, 123–124, 151, 190
Anticipation guides, 137–143
Antonyms, 64
Aphorisms, 188
Assessment, 3

B

Benchmark School, 11

C

Causal triads, 190–191
Center for Applied Special Technology (CAST), 21
Charts
    advantages, 125
    examples in teaching, 124, 136
    tips for using, 127
    types, 125–126
    within reading guides, 132
Choral reading, 28
Classwide peer tutoring, 30
Clock partners, 27–28
Cloze, 157–165, 189
Cloze Venns, 157–165
Compare-Contrast, 9–10
Comprehension
    lesson formats, 87–94
    subskill approaches, 86, 115
    teaching principles, 85–86

Concept sorts, 68–69
Connotations, 65
Critical questions, 98, 100

D

Decoding
    stage of development, 2, 3
    strategies, 7–21
    teaching principles, 7–8
Directed Reading Activity (DRA), 87–88, 94, 117
Directed Reading-Thinking Activity (DR-TA), 88–89, 94, 191
Drop Everything and Read (DEAR), 31

E

Echo reading, 28
Elaboration, 189
Electronic books, 19–21
Emergent literacy, 1

F

Feature analysis, 37–44, 70, 126–127
Fix-up strategies, 118
Fluency
    stage of development, 2, 3
    strategies, 25–32
    teaching principles, 25

G

Graphs, 45
Graphic organizers, 45–58, 70, 123, 149, 150, 154
Guess My Category, 68
Guided notes, 130–131
Guided Reading and Summarizing Procedure (GRASP), 155
Guided Reading in Textual Settings (GRITS), 117, 149–152

H

Headline writing, 189
Hypothesizing, 190

I

Imaging, 120–122
Independent reading level, 20
Induced Imaging, 120
Inferential questions, 97–98, 100

J

Juniper Garden Children's Project, 30

K

K-W-L, 90–93, 117

L

Labeled picture, 45, 49, 123
Learning the new, 2
Levels of questions, 97–99
Listening level, 19–20
Listen-Read-Discuss, 94, 117, 146
List-Group-Label, 66–69, 155
Literal questions, 97, 100, 103

M

Maze, 189–190
Mini-mysteries, 188

N

National Assessment of Educational Progress (NAEP), 1

O

Onset, 10

P

Paired reading, 26
Paired repeated reading, 26
Phonics, 9–16
Phonics word sorts, 12–16, 68–69
Picture interpretation, 188
Plays, 28
Possible sentences, 80–81
Prosody, 28
Puzzlers, 180–187

Q

Question-Answer Relationships (QARs), 100–102, 144
Question clusters, 86, 103–105
  bottom-up, 103
  clarifying, 104–105
  extending, 105
  slicing, 105
  top-down, 103–104
Questioning the Author (QtA), 108–112

R

Reading guides, 85, 117, 130, 131, 132–136, 137, 149, 150, 152
Reciprocal Questioning (ReQuest), 106–107
Reciprocal teaching, 124, 144–148
Repeated readings, 26
Riddles, 166–179

S

Secret codes, 189
Self-selected reading, 31–32
Semantic map, 45, 59, 59–61, 80
Semantic scales, 64–65
Semantic web, 45, 59
Sequencing comics, 189
Sidebars, 117
Silly questions, 78–79
Spider diagram, 59–60
Sociogram, 45, 49–50
SQ3R, 116
Stages of reading development, 1–3
Story problems, 188
Story starters, 191
Summaries
  in reciprocal teaching, 144
  writing, 86, 153–156
Supported text, 19
Survey technique, 116
Syllogisms, 189

T

Tables, 126
Tape-recorded text, 17–18
Teaching with Analogies (TWA), 123–124
Think-alouds, 86, 118–119, 149, 150, 152
Time lines, 45, 47, 50, 123
Treasure hunts, 188
Tree diagram, 45, 47, 50–53
Twenty questions, 188–189

U

Uninterrupted Sustained Silent Reading (USSR), 31

V

Venn diagram, 45, 47, 54–58, 62–63, 157–165

Vocabulary
    strategies, 37–81
    teaching principles, 35–36
Vocabulary clusters, 70–77
Vocabulary Venns, 62–63

W

Walk-throughs, 116–117, 149, 150, 151
Who-Wants-But-So, 155–156
Word sorts
    concept, 68–69
    open and closed, 14–15, 69
    phonics, 12–16, 68–69
Word walls, 10–11
Writing blurbs, 190
Writing morals, 190
Writing inferential questions, 191

Easter Seals
DISABILITY SERVICES

November 2015

Gerbera Daisy © Kenliang Wong

Easter Seals Dixon Center identifies and addresses gaps in services for returning military and their families, who need access to meaningful employment, health care and education. From children and adults living with disabilities, to military families looking to serve their communities, Easter Seals Dixon Center is committed to creating a world of inclusion, dignity, empowerment and independence.

Sunday	Monday	Tuesday	Wednesday	Thursday	Friday	Saturday
1 Daylight Saving Time Ends (Set clock back one hour)	**2**	**3** Election Day	**4**	**5**	**6**	**7**
8	**9**	**10**	**11** Veterans Day	**12**	**13**	**14**
15	**16**	**17**	**18**	**19**	**20**	**21**
22	**23**	**24**	**25**	**26** Thanksgiving Day	**27**	**28**
29	**30**					

OCTOBER 2015

S	M	T	W	T	F	S
				1	2	3
4	5	6	7	8	9	10
11	12	13	14	15	16	17
18	19	20	21	22	23	24
25	26	27	28	29	30	31

DECEMBER 2015

S	M	T	W	T	F	S
		1	2	3	4	5
6	7	8	9	10	11	12
13	14	15	16	17	18	19
20	21	22	23	24	25	26
27	28	29	30	31		

To learn more about what Easter Seals Dixon Center is doing to support veterans, visit eastersealsdixoncenter.org.

easterseals.com

The History of Easter Seals

Tragedy Leads to Inspiration

1919

Elyria, Ohio, businessman Edgar Allen founded the National Society for Crippled Children in 1919, the first organization of its kind. Following a personal tragedy, he dedicated his life to improving access to health care for children with disabilities.

The Birth of the Seal

1934

In the spring of 1934, the National Society for Crippled Children launched its first Easter "seal" fundraising campaign. Donors placed the seals on envelopes to show support for the organization's vital services.

Easter Seals Emerges

1967

"Easter Seals" was formally adopted as the organization's name after overwhelming public support for the annual "seal" campaign became synonymous with the organization's work.

Helping Pass the ADA

1990

Easter Seals advocated for passing the landmark Americans with Disabilities Act (ADA) into law. The ADA prohibits discrimination against anyone who has a mental or physical disability—guaranteeing the civil rights of people with disabilities.

Easter Seals Goes Global

2004

Easter Seals welcomed its first international partner, Ability First Australia, to its network of affiliates.

Spotlighting Autism Services

2007

One of the nation's leading providers of services and support for people with autism, Easter Seals began raising public awareness about families affected by autism ... and how they can find help, hope and answers at Easter Seals.

Dedicated Easter Seals Dixon Center

2012

Easter Seals Dixon Center identifies and addresses gaps in services for military families who need access to meaningful employment, health care and education.

Easter Seals Today

2015

Easter Seals offers help, hope and answers for children and adults with autism, developmental disabilities, physical disabilities and other special needs — and for their families — in communities across the United States. We create life-changing solutions through therapy, training, education and support services so people with disabilities can live, learn, work, play and contribute to society.

MAKING A DIFFERENCE FOR QUINN

© Chris Jenkins photography

Six-year-old Quinn lights up a room with his smile and natural charm. He loves to laugh and works hard to keep up with his twin sister, Emma, as well as his older sisters, Grace, 10, and Vivian, 8.

He has come so far since he was 4 months old, when his mother, Sarah, noticed his eyes didn't look right. He also wasn't developing at the same pace as his twin.

After many tests, doctors found Quinn has a neurological condition and may have had a stroke in utero. "We were devastated," Sarah recalls, saying those days were like "swimming without a raft."

Then the family came to Easter Seals. "They gave us hope," Sarah says. "They said the brain is an amazing thing — that the right therapy could make a difference."

Since then, Quinn has received physical, occupational, speech and nutrition therapy at Easter Seals. He still faces many challenges, but he also has made great strides toward becoming more independent.

For example, since he is unable to communicate verbally, Easter Seals is teaching Quinn to use sign language and an assistive technology device customized just for him. He also is working on dressing and feeding himself. Best of all, Quinn recently mastered walking with the aid of a walker!

Derek, Quinn's father, is amazed by the extent Easter Seals goes to support his son and family.

"They're an amazing resource," he says. "It's quite a thing to have advocates for your child, other than yourself. It's pretty neat to see."

By supporting Easter Seals, you're making a difference for children and adults like Quinn. We appreciate your generosity.

Learn more about an Easter Seals near you!

Get our free monthly email newsletter featuring disability news and event information in your area.

Subscribe now at: easterseals.com/subscribe

OCTOBER 2015

Dahlias (Tamburo variety) © VisionsPictures/MindenPictures

Easter Seals offers programs such as adult day services, in-home support, community mobility options, wellness programs and support for family caregivers that help people live independently and of their own choosing for as long as possible.

	SEPTEMBER 2015							NOVEMBER 2015					
S	M	T	W	T	F	S	S	M	T	W	T	F	S
		1	2	3	4	5	1	2	3	4	5	6	7
6	7	8	9	10	11	12	8	9	10	11	12	13	14
13	14	15	16	17	18	19	15	16	17	18	19	20	21
20	21	22	23	24	25	26	22	23	24	25	26	27	28
27	28	29	30				29	30					

Sunday	Monday	Tuesday	Wednesday	Thursday	Friday	Saturday
				1	2	3
4	5	6	7	8	9	10
11	12 Columbus Day	13	14	15	16	17
18	19	20	21	22	23	24
25	26	27	28	29	30	31 Halloween

How do you decide what is best for an aging parent?
For a free guide, visit easterseals.com/conversations

easterseals.com

JANUARY 2015

Clematis © VisionsPictures/MindenPictures

Today, as many as 1 in every 88 children are diagnosed with Autism Spectrum Disorder (ASD) — making ASD the fastest-growing developmental disability.

Sunday	Monday	Tuesday	Wednesday	Thursday	Friday	Saturday
				1 New Year's Day	2	3
4	5	6	7	8	9	10
11	12	13	14	15	16	17
18	19 Martin Luther King, Jr. Day (Observed)	20	21	22	23	24
25	26	27	28	29	30	31

DECEMBER 2014

S	M	T	W	T	F	S
	1	2	3	4	5	6
7	8	9	10	11	12	13
14	15	16	17	18	19	20
21	22	23	24	25	26	27
28	29	30	31			

FEBRUARY 2015

S	M	T	W	T	F	S
1	2	3	4	5	6	7
8	9	10	11	12	13	14
15	16	17	18	19	20	21
22	23	24	25	26	27	28

Consider becoming a monthly donor.
Visit easterseals.com/sustainer

easterseals.com

Easter Seals
DISABILITY SERVICES

FEBRUARY 2015

Respite programs provide relief for families and primary caregivers of individuals with special needs or disabilities. Respite care enhances family health by offering necessary physical care and recreational activities for children, veterans and older adults with special needs, while offering caregivers a well-deserved break.

Cinquefoil (Flambeau variety) © VisionsPictures/MindenPictures

Sunday	Monday	Tuesday	Wednesday	Thursday	Friday	Saturday
1	2 Groundhog Day	3	4	5	6	7
8	9	10	11 Lincoln's Birthday	12	13 Valentine's Day	14
15 Presidents' Day Washington's Birthday (Observed)	16	17	18 Ash Wednesday	19	20	21
22	23	24	25	26	27	28

JANUARY 2015

S	M	T	W	T	F	S
				1	2	3
4	5	6	7	8	9	10
11	12	13	14	15	16	17
18	19	20	21	22	23	24
25	26	27	28	29	30	31

MARCH 2015

S	M	T	W	T	F	S
1	2	3	4	5	6	7
8	9	10	11	12	13	14
15	16	17	18	19	20	21
22	23	24	25	26	27	28
29	30	31				

Are you a caregiver for a child, veteran or aging loved one? Visit easterseals.com/caregiver for information and support.

easterseals.com

Easter Seals
DISABILITY SERVICES

SEPTEMBER 2015

For 40 years, the Individuals with Disabilities Education Act (IDEA) has guaranteed a free and appropriate public education for all students, as well as access to early intervention and preschool programs for children with disabilities.

Sunday	Monday	Tuesday	Wednesday	Thursday	Friday	Saturday
		1	**2**	**3**	**4**	**5**
6	**7** Labor Day	**8**	**9**	**10**	**11** Patriot Day	**12**
13 Rosh Hashanah (Begins at sundown the day before)	**14**	**15**	**16**	**17** Citizenship Day	**18**	**19**
20	**21**	**22**	**23** Yom Kippur (Begins at sundown the day before) First Day of Autumn	**24**	**25**	**26**
27	**28**	**29**	**30**			

Grandparents Day

Get our disability awareness curriculum for elementary students. Visit easterseals.com/friendswhocare

easterseals.com

AUGUST 2015						
S	M	T	W	T	F	S
						1
2	3	4	5	6	7	8
9	10	11	12	13	14	15
16	17	18	19	20	21	22
23/30	24/31	25	26	27	28	29

OCTOBER 2015						
S	M	T	W	T	F	S
				1	2	3
4	5	6	7	8	9	10
11	12	13	14	15	16	17
18	19	20	21	22	23	24
25	26	27	28	29	30	31

Easter Seals
DISABILITY SERVICES

AUGUST 2015

Medical rehabilitation offers people with disabilities the opportunity to live up to their physical potential, achieve independence and participate in their communities.

Lupine © VisionsPictures/MindenPictures

JULY 2015

S	M	T	W	T	F	S
			1	2	3	4
5	6	7	8	9	10	11
12	13	14	15	16	17	18
19	20	21	22	23	24	25
26	27	28	29	30	31	

SEPTEMBER 2015

S	M	T	W	T	F	S
		1	2	3	4	5
6	7	8	9	10	11	12
13	14	15	16	17	18	19
20	21	22	23	24	25	26
27	28	29	30			

Sunday	Monday	Tuesday	Wednesday	Thursday	Friday	Saturday
						1
2	3	4	5	6	7	8
9	10	11	12	13	14	15
16	17	18	19	20	21	22
23	24	25	26	27	28	29
30	31					

Walk with Easter Seals! Find a family-friendly walk near you at walkwithme.org

easterseals.com

Easter Seals
DISABILITY SERVICES®

MARCH 2015

Camping and recreational programs for children and adults with disabilities offer unique opportunities to make friends, find inner talents and strengths and just have fun. Camping programs help build self-esteem and confidence through new and challenging experiences.

Common Meadowfoam © Geoff Du Feu/MaxxImages

Sunday	Monday	Tuesday	Wednesday	Thursday	Friday	Saturday
1	2	3	4	5	6	7
8 Daylight Saving Time Begins (Set clock ahead one hour)	9	10	11 ○	12	13	14
15	16	17 St. Patrick's Day	18	19	20 First Day of Spring ◐	21
22	23	24	25	26	27 ●	28
29 Palm Sunday	30	31				

Purim (Begins at sundown the day before) — on 5

FEBRUARY 2015
S	M	T	W	T	F	S
1	2	3	4	5	6	7
8	9	10	11	12	13	14
15	16	17	18	19	20	21
22	23	24	25	26	27	28

APRIL 2015
S	M	T	W	T	F	S
			1	2	3	4
5	6	7	8	9	10	11
12	13	14	15	16	17	18
19	20	21	22	23	24	25
26	27	28	29	30		

Consider the tax advantages of a Gift Annuity.
Visit easterseals.com/annuity

easterseals.com

Easter Seals
DISABILITY SERVICES®

APRIL —2015

Tulip (Sunset Miami) © Julianne Eggers/Corbis

People living with Autism Spectrum Disorder — at any age — are capable of making significant progress through personalized interventions and therapy; and can and do lead meaningful lives. April is Autism Awareness Month. Please help raise awareness of services and treatments available for families.

Sunday	Monday	Tuesday	Wednesday	Thursday	Friday	Saturday
			1	**2**	**3** Good Friday / First Day of Passover (Begins at sundown the day before)	**4**
5 Easter Sunday	**6**	**7**	**8**	**9**	**10**	**11**
12 Orthodox Easter	**13**	**14**	**15**	**16**	**17**	**18**
19	**20**	**21**	**22** Earth Day / Administrative Professionals Day	**23** Arbor Day	**24**	**25**
26	**27**	**28**	**29**	**30**		

MARCH 2015

S	M	T	W	T	F	S
1	2	3	4	5	6	7
8	9	10	11	12	13	14
15	16	17	18	19	20	21
22	23	24	25	26	27	28
29	30	31				

MAY 2015

S	M	T	W	T	F	S
					1	2
3	4	5	6	7	8	9
10	11	12	13	14	15	16
17	18	19	20	21	22	23
24/31	25	26	27	28	29	30

Is your child or grandchild developing on time? Take the Ages & Stages Questionnaire® at easterseals.com/ASQ

easterseals.com

Follow us on facebook.com/easterseals
and twitter.com/easter_seals

Easter Seals
DISABILITY SERVICES

JULY — 2015

The Americans with Disabilities Act (ADA) was signed into law on July 26, 1990. 25 years later, it continues to protect people with disabilities from discrimination in private-sector employment and provides equal access to public accommodations, public services, transportation and telecommunications.

Spring Star Flower © Graham Rice/GardenPhotos.com

JUNE 2015

S	M	T	W	T	F	S
	1	2	3	4	5	6
7	8	9	10	11	12	13
14	15	16	17	18	19	20
21	22	23	24	25	26	27
28	29	30				

Sunday	Monday	Tuesday	Wednesday	Thursday	Friday	Saturday
			1	2	3 Independence Day	4
5	6	7	8	9	10	11
12	13	14	15	16	17	18
19	20	21	22	23	24	25
26	27	28	29	30	31	

AUGUST 2015

S	M	T	W	T	F	S
						1
2	3	4	5	6	7	8
9	10	11	12	13	14	15
16	17	18	19	20	21	22
23/30	24/31	25	26	27	28	29

easterseals.com

Mums © Bonnie Sue Rauch

JUNE 2015

Every year, more than one million children with unidentified disabilities enter school with learning and health issues that put them far behind their peers. Early identification through an annual screening and access to therapy services can make a life-changing difference for every child under age 5.

Sunday	Monday	Tuesday	Wednesday	Thursday	Friday	Saturday
	1	2	3	4	5	6
7	8	9	10	11	12	13
Flag Day 14	15	16	17	**First Day of Ramadan** (Begins at sundown the day before) 18	19	20
Father's Day **First Day of Summer** 21	22	23	24	25	26	27
28	29	30				

The first 5 years are critical. Check a child's development with the Ages and Stages Questionnaire® at easterseals.com/ASQ

MAY 2015

S	M	T	W	T	F	S
					1	2
3	4	5	6	7	8	9
10	11	12	13	14	15	16
17	18	19	20	21	22	23
24/31	25	26	27	28	29	30

JULY 2015

S	M	T	W	T	F	S
			1	2	3	4
5	6	7	8	9	10	11
12	13	14	15	16	17	18
19	20	21	22	23	24	25
26	27	28	29	30	31	

Easter Seals
DISABILITY SERVICES

MAY 2015

Job training and employment services benefit people with disabilities, older workers and veterans, providing first job preparation, assistance returning to work or transition services post-deployment. Through employment, individuals gain self-esteem and social skills as productive members of their communities, and employers gain dedicated, reliable, well-trained staff.

Dutch Crocus © Justus de Cuveland/MaxImages

Sunday	Monday	Tuesday	Wednesday	Thursday	Friday	Saturday
					1	**2**
3	**4**	**5**	**6**	**7**	**8**	**9**
10 Mother's Day	**11**	**12**	**13**	**14**	**15** Armed Forces Day	**16**
17	**18**	**19**	**20**	**21** National Maritime Day	**22**	**23**
24	**25** Memorial Day (Observed)	**26**	**27**	**28**	**29**	**30**
31						

APRIL 2015
S	M	T	W	T	F	S
			1	2	3	4
5	6	7	8	9	10	11
12	13	14	15	16	17	18
19	20	21	22	23	24	25
26	27	28	29	30		

JUNE 2015
S	M	T	W	T	F	S
	1	2	3	4	5	6
7	8	9	10	11	12	13
14	15	16	17	18	19	20
21	22	23	24	25	26	27
28	29	30				

See all the great reasons to hire a veteran at easterseals.com/hireveterans

easterseals.com